21 Sensational
Patchwork
Bags

Susan
Briscoe

D&C
David and Charles

For Guy, who says I still don't have enough bags!

A DAVID & CHARLES BOOK
Copyright © David & Charles Limited 2006, 2007

David & Charles is an F+W Publications Inc. company
4700 East Galbraith Road
Cincinnati, OH 45236

First published in the UK in 2006
First US paperback 2006
Reprinted 2006 and 2007
First UK paperback edition 2007

Text and designs copyright © Susan Briscoe 2006

ISBN-13: 978-0-7153-2232-1 hardback
ISBN-10: 0-7153-2232-X hardback

ISBN-13: 978-0-7153-2464-6 paperback
ISBN-10: 0-7153-2464-0 paperback

Printed in China by Shenzen Donnelley Printing Co., Ltd
for David & Charles
Brunel House, Newton Abbot, Devon

Executive Editor Cheryl Brown
Editor Ame Verso
Project Editor Linda Clements
Head of Design Prudence Rogers
Designer Louise Prentice
Photography Karl Adamson and Kim Sayer
Production Controller Ros Napper

Visit our website at www.davidandcharles.co.uk

David & Charles books are available from all good bookshops; alternatively you can contact our Orderline
on 0870 9908222 or write to us at FREEPOST EX2 110, D&C Direct, Newton Abbot, TQ12 4ZZ (no stamp
required UK only); US customers call 800-289-0963 and Canadian customers call 800-840-5220.

Photograph on previous page
*This collection of attractive but very practical bags was specially designed for 'quilters on the go' and features
evocative sepia and taupe country prints with photographs printed on fabrics. From left to right: Log Cabin
Saddlebag (page 48); Sepia Tringle (page 73); Magical Memories Sack (page 89) and Quilter's Pocket Book (page 20).*

CONTENTS

INTRODUCTION

I had great fun dreaming up designs for my last patchwork bag book, *21 Terrific Patchwork Bags*, but had far too many ideas for one book so *21 Sensational Patchwork Bags* presents a further exciting selection of great bags for all occasions – for work and play. There are bags for shopping, walking, quilting, partying, studying, giving as gifts, glamorous nights out, casual nights in or just to go with your favourite jeans. They make perfect presents for friends and family – so much quicker to make than a bed quilt and satisfying to complete.

Once again, I have included plenty of bags where you can try out some new techniques or return to your favourites, whether you are coming to this absorbing craft for the first time or building on existing patchwork and quilting skills. There are designs suitable for using up your fabric scraps, leftover strips and wadding pieces, or co-ordinated sets perfect for those fat quarter bundles and charm packs that we quilters just can't resist. You can even include heavier fabrics, like denim and faux suede. Several bags make use of construction methods that will be familiar from quilt making, such as bias-bound edges. Style and practicality can go together and your bags will certainly be unique!

Favourite patchwork blocks get a country-style treatment with woven plaids or take on a new look with sparkly metallic fabrics or bright batiks. Victorian Crazy Patchwork gets traditional and modern interpretations, with fancy stitching by hand or machine. Log Cabin, so useful for using up fabric strips, makes a number of appearances, with off-centre and half Log Cabin variations explored too. Several bags feature ideas for using personalized fabrics you have created yourself, by rubber-stamping on fabric or up-to-date computer photo printing. Since *21 Terrific Patchwork Bags* was published, bag fittings such as metal zips, D-rings, clips and ready-made handles are more widely available in quilt shops, so I've used these where appropriate. There's scope for using ethnic and retro fabrics, plus those special buttons, braids and cords that we squirrel away.

Happy bag-making!

Using This Book

The following are useful points about using this book, even for experienced quilters, so please read before making any project. If you need further information on equipment, materials and techniques will find all you need to know in the section beginning on page 90.

✓ Fabric pieces and patchwork blocks are given *without* seam allowances, unless stated otherwise, so add a ¼in seam allowance all round where not already included. Add ½in seam allowance to edges of openings where zips will be inserted.

✓ Wadding (batting) and backing fabric sizes are cut larger than required and trimmed to size after quilting.

✓ Actual sizes are given for cord, braid, zips and so on. There is no need to add on any extra allowance.

✓ 'Machine sew' means with straight stitch, unless otherwise stated. Start and finish all bag seams by reverse stitching for ½in.

✓ Where possible patchwork blocks in the projects have been supplied actual size but do check the individual diagrams for the size required.

✓ Press seams after sewing each stage of patchwork and bag assembly. Where patchwork is sewn to a plain panel, the seams are pressed away from the patchwork.

✓ Illustrations of the stitches used can be found in the Stitch Library on page 112.

✓ Alternative patchwork blocks are supplied in the Block Library on pages 116 and 117.

THE PROJECTS

This book has an exciting range of different bags for you to choose from and they are shown here (not to scale) to help you select your first project. The easier bags are at the beginning of the book, with more complicated ones later on. Of course, there's nothing to stop you giving your bag a totally unique look by using different fabrics and trims or by changing the patchwork block used. You could even use up a 'UFO', the quilter's term for an Un-Finished Object! Whichever project you start with, you are sure to have great fun stitching your patchwork bag.

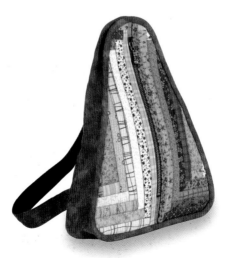

QUILTER'S PORTFOLIO

A portfolio like this is one of the first items made by my patchwork students and is ideal for carrying a cutting mat and ruler. The two outer pockets, perfect for sketchbooks, are made from a giant half Log Cabin block, cut and rearranged to extend the panel at the sides. Cutting the fabrics across the stripes makes the patchwork look more complex. The main bag is made in flat sections, just like making a small quilt – the sides even have bias-bound edges.

This striped and spotted bag will carry your quilting essentials – and in colourful style too. Press studs keep equipment safe in the side pockets. Ready-made leather bag handles give the bag a really professional look but can be replaced with other straps (see page 110). Team it with the Pudding Bag (page 32) to turn heads at your quilt class or workshop.

YOU WILL NEED

(Unless otherwise stated, add seam allowances to fabric and wadding sizes – see page 5)

- One half Log Cabin foundation-pieced patchwork panel 25in square for pocket, from:
  - assorted 2in wide strips up to 25½in long (includes seam allowances)
  - one 3½in square (includes seam allowances)

- Two 19in x 25in pieces of two different printed fabrics for bag panel (includes seam allowances)
- Calico backing fabric pieces:
  - one 26in square for Log Cabin foundation
  - one 38in x 26in for bag panel
- 2oz cotton wadding (batting) 38in x 26in

- Lining fabric pieces:
  - one 25in square for bag pocket
  - one 35in x 25in for bag lining
- Two ready-made bag handles 27in long
- Two 19½in x 2in bias-cut strips (see page 107) for double bias binding (includes seam allowances)
- Two large press-stud fasteners
- Sewing and quilting threads to tone with patchwork

MAKING THE PATCHWORK

1 Begin by making one half Log Cabin block, finished size 25½in square (including seam allowances). Draw the pattern shown in **Fig 1** on to the 26in square piece of calico (this is the foundation). Begin drawing with the two longest lines 2in from the outer edge and draw the other lines parallel to these at 1½in intervals. Starting with the 3in corner square, machine sew the patchwork to the foundation, sewing 1½in wide strips to alternate sides of the square, lining up the edges of the strips with the lines on the foundation. Sew light strips on one half of the Log Cabin and darker ones on the other for a shaded effect (see Log Cabin page 102).

2 With right sides together, machine sew the two different printed 19in x 25in pieces along one long side only and press the seam to one side. Using the wadding (batting) and backing fabric, make a quilt sandwich (see page 104), and machine quilt a grid pattern (see Machine quilting page 104). Horizontal lines are 1in apart, vertical lines are ½in apart. Alternatively, free-motion machine quilt in a stipple pattern or hand quilt. Trim the panel to measure 35in x 24½in. Overlock or zigzag the edge, keeping the stitch width less than ¼in. The bag panel is now complete. Right sides together, sew the 25 x 25in lining panel to the shorter ends of the bag panel, and turn right sides out.

IDEA

TO MAKE A QUILTER'S PORTFOLIO TO HOLD A LARGER OR SMALLER CUTTING MAT, BEGIN WITH THE OUTER FABRIC 1½IN–2IN LARGER ALL ROUND, AS DENSE QUILTING WILL DECREASE THE SIZE. TRIM TO ¾IN LARGER THAN YOUR MAT SIZE AFTER QUILTING FOR AN AVERAGE FIT OR ½IN LARGER FOR A REALLY SNUG FIT.

Fig 1 *Corner Log Cabin patchwork for side pocket*

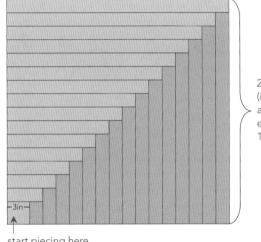

25½in square (including seam allowances) – each strip is 1½in wide

3in

start piecing here

TIP

CUT THE LOG CABIN STRIPS TO LENGTH AS YOU SEW, KEEPING THE LONGER PIECES LEFT OVER FROM THE FIRST FEW STRIPS TO USE TOWARDS THE OUTSIDE OF THE BLOCK; THIS IS MORE ECONOMICAL THAN CUTTING SEVERAL SHORT PIECES FROM THE SAME LONG STRIP, ONLY TO NEED TO CUT EXTRA LONG STRIPS LATER ON.

CONSTRUCTING THE BAG

3 *Making the pocket panel:* With reference to **Fig 2,** use the bag panel as a guide to cut the Log Cabin bag pocket to size. Match the corners of the Log Cabin block with the centres of the short sides of the bag panel. Mark and trim off the pocket panel triangle points and cut both triangles in half again, as shown by the red dashed lines on the diagram. Using the pocket panel and pieces as a guide, cut the 25in square lining fabric to match. If you wish, you could machine sew the cut bias edges of the pocket panel to stabilize them.

Fig 2
Making
the pocket
panel

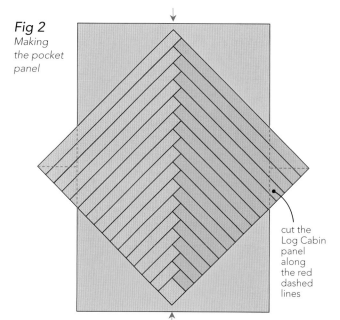

cut the
Log Cabin
panel
along
the red
dashed
lines

match the corners of the Log Cabin panel
to the centre of the quilted bag panel
before cutting

4 Pin a corresponding piece of lining fabric to each triangle, along one short side only, machine sew with a ¼in seam and press the seam to one side, as shown. This seam will be at the top edge of the pocket when the bag is complete. You need to make a left-hand and a right-hand triangle for each side of the bag, so check which way the patchwork strips are running on each triangle before you sew – see the picture with Step 6 overleaf to arrange each piece in the right place.

IDEA

THE LIGHT AND DARK TONES IN THE LOG CABIN
BLOCKS CAN BE REPLACED WITH A DIFFERENT
CONTRAST – SHINY SILK AND MATTE COTTON,
LARGE-SCALE PRINTS AND PLAINS, OR TWO
CONTRASTING COLOURS, SUCH AS BLUE AND
ORANGE. STRIPS CAN ALSO BE PIECED.

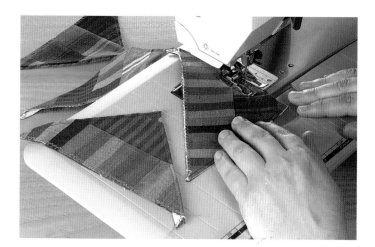

5 Press each triangle piece in half, so the lining is behind the patchwork. Machine sew the bias edges together and top stitch along the fold, ⅛in from the edge.

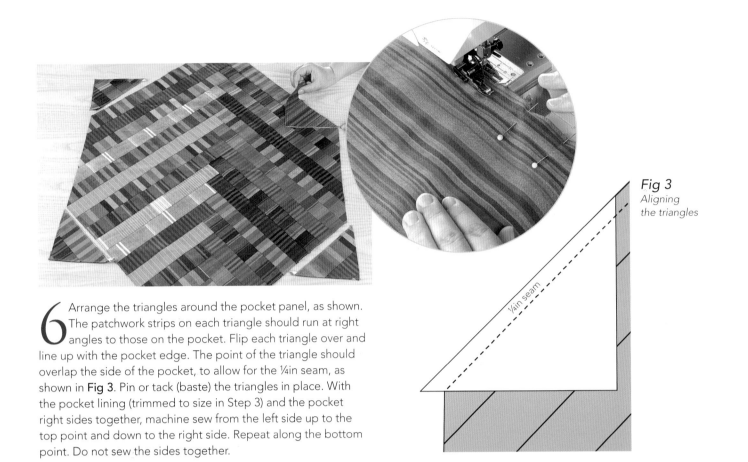

Fig 3
Aligning the triangles

¼in seam

6 Arrange the triangles around the pocket panel, as shown. The patchwork strips on each triangle should run at right angles to those on the pocket. Flip each triangle over and line up with the pocket edge. The point of the triangle should overlap the side of the pocket, to allow for the ¼in seam, as shown in **Fig 3**. Pin or tack (baste) the triangles in place. With the pocket lining (trimmed to size in Step 3) and the pocket right sides together, machine sew from the left side up to the top point and down to the right side. Repeat along the bottom point. Do not sew the sides together.

7 Bag out, by turning the pocket panel right side out through the gap in one side. Clip the top points and make sure they are fully turned out. Press the edges around the pocket panel and top stitch around the panel, ⅛in from the edge. The pocket panel is now complete.

IDEA

FOR A QUICK AND EASY QUILTER'S PORTFOLIO, MAKE THE BAG WITHOUT ANY OUTER POCKETS. YOU COULD RECYCLE AN UNFINISHED QUILT TOP!

8 *Completing the bag outer:* Place the bag panel right side up and centre the pocket panel on top. Pin together and then machine sew the two panels together as shown, stitching along the sides only, ⅛in from the edge. The bag outer is now complete. Fold the bag outer in half and mark the fold line at the bottom of the bag. Open the panel out flat again, pin along the fold line and sew across the bottom of the bag to separate one pocket from the other. For extra strength, use a straight stretch stitch on the machine.

9 Sew the outer halves of the large press studs to the inside of the pocket's top points, setting them about ⅛in from the edge and taking care to sew through the lining only. Line up and sew the inner halves of the press studs, this time taking care to sew through the bag outer only. Fold the bag in half again, line up the sides, pin and machine sew the sides together, stitching ⅛in from the edge. Overlock or zigzag the edge, keeping the stitch width less than ¼in.

10 *Sewing the binding:* Using the bias-cut strip, make double bias binding (see Making and attaching bindings page 107). Pin and machine sew the binding along both sides of the bag, being careful not to stretch the binding, and overlapping the ends by ½in. When the machine stitching is complete, fold the bias binding over and slipstitch (hem stitch) it in place along the bag sides, folding the ends over before sewing along the length.

TIP

PLACE YOUR DOMINANT HAND BETWEEN THE LINING AND THE BAG PANEL WHEN SEWING THE SECOND PART OF THE PRESS STUD IN PLACE, SEPARATING THE LINING AND OUTER PANEL, SO THERE'S NO RISK OF SEWING THROUGH THE LINING.

11 To complete your bag, hand sew the ready-made bag straps to the top of the bag pocket, with the bottom edge of the straps 6½in from the point at the top of the pocket. If you are using slightly longer or shorter straps, you will need to reposition them.

◻ BATIK BUTTERFLY BAG

My student Pat Morris made the prototype of this portfolio with a horizontal ruler pocket but we realized a diagonal pocket with a button and loop fastening would not only be neater but the ruler can't slip out easily! The pocket fits a quilter's ruler up to 6½in wide and 24in long. When making this version I used up the little triangle squares left over from making the Flying Geese on the Batik Bottle Tidy (page 62) as part of the patchwork, adding more batiks and different quilting patterns. The bag is the same size as the original Quilter's Portfolio, 18in x 24in.

TUCK-IN SHOULDER BAG

This roomy bag has two patchwork flaps – one to
tuck in and one to display – both edged with double
bias binding. Turn it around to suit your mood! I used
distressed denim and the wrong side of checked and
striped cotton flannels to remind me of favourite jeans
and shirts, complete with jeans buttons on the adjustable
strap and quilting in shaded yellow ochre thread for a
washed-out look. Woven plaids continue in the lining.

This versatile bag has two different
flaps – will you choose to wear it
with the sampler flap showing or
like this, with the plain squares on
show, perfect for a collection of club
souvenir badges (pins)? There's a
square each for up to 36 badges.

YOU WILL NEED

(Unless otherwise stated, add seam allowances to all fabric and wadding sizes – see page 5)

- One 12in square patchwork panel from four 6in blocks:
  – one 6in square Birds in Flight block
  – one 6in square Prairie Flower block
  – two 6in square Four-Patch Star blocks
- One 12in square checkerboard patchwork panel from thirty-six 2in squares
- Two 16in x 2in patchwork insert strips from eight 2in squares

- Denim pieces (seam allowances included):
  – one 28in x 18½in for bag straps and top
  – one 20½in x 16½in for main bag panel
- Backing fabric pieces:
  – two 13in squares for patchwork panels
  – two 17in x 3in for patchwork insert strips
- 2oz cotton wadding (batting) pieces:
  – two 13in squares
  – two 17in x 3in
- Lining fabric pieces (seam allowances included):
  – one 71½in x 16½in for bag

- two 12½in squares for flaps
- Two 3in x 4in pieces of lightweight iron-on interfacing
- Two 2in x 38in bias-cut fabric strips
- Four jeans buttons or others of your choice
- Sewing and quilting threads to tone with patchwork
- Shaded machine embroidery or jeans thread
- Machine embroidery needle suitable for machine embroidery or jeans thread
- 2½in diameter circle template

MAKING THE PATCHWORK

1 Begin by making one Birds in Flight, one Prairie Flower and two Four-Patch Star 6in blocks (see Block Library, page 116). Each block is made from an assortment of 2in strips, squares and triangle squares (finished sizes) – refer to Patchwork Techniques beginning on page 97. Machine sew the four blocks together into one patchwork panel, alternating the designs, as shown in **Fig 1**. This is the first bag flap.

2 Make one checkerboard patchwork panel (the second bag flap) from thirty-six 2in squares and two insert strips of eight 2in squares (finished sizes). Use a random layout, as shown in **Fig 2**.

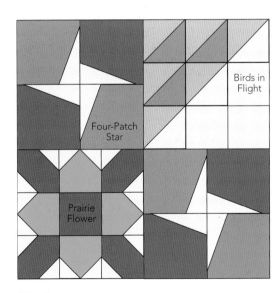

Fig 1 First flap – patchwork layout of the four blocks

Fig 2 Second flap – patchwork layout of panel

TIP

CUT 2½IN STRIPS AND CUT SQUARES FROM THE STRIPS FOR THE SQUARES IN STEP 1. USE UP THE SCRAPS TO MAKE THE CHECKERBOARD AND STRIPS OF SQUARES.

3 With the wadding (batting) and backing, make a quilt sandwich (see page 104) for each panel and then machine quilt (page 104). Quilt each panel in the ditch (along the patchwork seams), then quilt the patterns shown in **Fig 3** (first flap) and **Fig 4** (second flap) with shaded machine embroidery or jeans thread, following the dotted lines. Quilt the two insert strips with simple zigzags.

⊡ Constructing the Bag

4 Using the 28in x 18½in piece of denim, cut out the bag straps and top sections (**Fig 5**). Note, the height of the top section is smaller on one side of the bag, to create a stepped effect where the patchwork inserts meet on the side seam. With the two patchwork inserts, machine sew one to the bottom edge of each strap/top section. Press towards the denim and topstitch through the seam allowance with shaded machine embroidery thread, stitching ⅛in from the seam. Machine sew the two complete strap/top sections to the 20½in x 16½in piece of denim, as shown in **Fig 6**. Press and topstitch as before. Use the completed bag panel as a pattern to cut out the lining fabric.

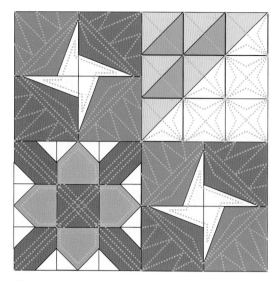

Fig 3 Quilting pattern for the first flap

Fig 4 Quilting pattern for the second flap

Fig 5
Cutting out the bag straps and top sections in the most economical way. Save the coloured sections for your scrap stash

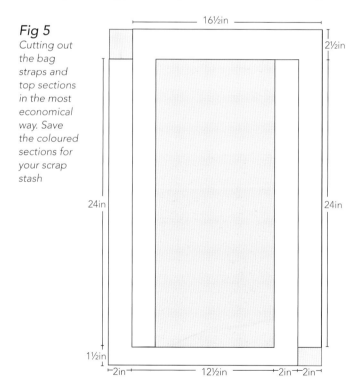

Idea

If your distressed denim has small holes or tears in it, just add a checked patch from the back before making up the bag. You could piece the bag panel from old jeans for a truly vintage look.

patchwork insert

Fig 6 Attaching the strap/top sections to the piece of denim

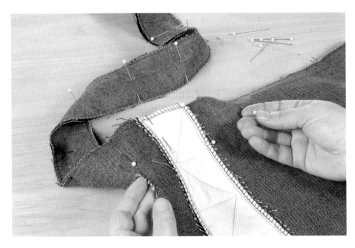

5 Fold the bag panel in half, right sides together. Line up the side edges and pin along the sides and strap. Machine sew and then press the seam open. Repeat for the other side seam. To reinforce the strap for the buttons and buttonholes, iron on the two pieces of interfacing to the wrong side of each end of the straps, setting them ¾in from the end of the strap. Note: the interfacing does not extend into the seam allowances.

6 With the bag wrong side out, fold a bottom corner point to form a right angle, with the side seam running into the point in the centre. Mark a line at right angles to the side seam, 2in from the point, then pin and machine sew across. Trim off the triangular flap of fabric and oversew or zigzag the raw edge. Repeat for the other corner.

7 Inserting the lining: Assemble the lining fabric the same way as the bag panel, following Steps 5 and 6, but leave a 6in gap unsewn in one side seam only, where it will be inside the bag. Turn the lining right side out and the bag wrong side out. Place the lining inside the bag and pin the lining to the bag along the straps only. Machine sew the lining to the bag along the straps, starting and finishing ¼in below the top edge of the bag.

8 Finishing the patchwork flaps: Using a 2½in circle template, trim the two bottom corners on each flap to a neat curve. Pin and sew one 12½in square of lining to the back of each flap, wrong sides together, and trim the bottom corners to match. Using the bias-cut strip, make double bias binding (see Making and attaching bindings, page 107). Pin and machine sew one binding strip around the edge of each flap, being careful not to stretch the binding. When the machine stitching is complete, fold the binding over and slipstitch it in place all around each flap.

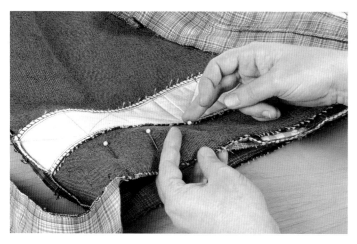

9 Slip the checkerboard flap inside the bag, through the gap left at the top on one side, between the lining and the bag outer, with the patchwork and the bag outer fabric right sides together. The flap will have almost disappeared between the lining and the bag. Line up the top edge of the flap with the top of the lining and bag outer. Pin together, starting at each end, and then machine sew together. Repeat for the other flap. I sewed the checkerboard flap to the side where the height of the top section is smaller, but the flaps can be sewn to either side.

10 Clip into the corners where the flaps are sewn to the top of the bag, being careful not to cut into the stitching. Clip the corners at the top of the straps. Bag out, by turning the bag right side out through the gap in the lining. Make sure the top corners on the straps are fully turned out. Press the edges all round the bag and topstitch through the seam allowances with shaded machine embroidery or jeans thread, stitching ⅛in from the edge along the straps and across where the flaps are joined to the bag. Slipstitch the lining closed.

IDEA

IF YOU ARE HAPPY WITH A FIXED STRAP LENGTH AND WANT SEWN-ON BUTTONS, OVERLAP AND STITCH THE STRAPS TOGETHER UNDER THE BUTTONS.

11 *Adding buttons and buttonholes:* Lay the bag down with both flaps laid out flat. Tuck the checkerboard flap inside the bag temporarily and fold the other flap over the top of the bag. Take the strap on the right and mark the positions for the buttons – the first two ¾in from the end and the second two 3½in from the end – each button centred either side of the strap seam. Attach the jeans buttons with their rivets, following the manufacturer's instructions. Alternatively, use stitched buttons. Overlap the strap on the left and use the position of the buttons to mark the positions for your buttonholes. Using the buttonhole attachment on your sewing machine, stitch the buttonholes and cut them open. Fasten the buttons through the buttonholes to finish the strap.

QUILTER'S POCKET BOOK

The perfect accessory for a quilt show visitor or
organized shopper, this neat little pocket book has
a place for everything you'll need readily to hand.
It closes with a snap fastener and the wrist strap
is removable. Made from sepia fabrics with elongated
quarter Log Cabin patchwork, it co-ordinates with the
bags on pages 48, 73 and 89. You can make your own
notebook for a personalized touch too!

You're sure to find many uses for this
handy pocket book: there are
pockets for fabric snippets,
colour inspiration notes
and shopping lists; there are
also smaller pockets to store
discount or club membership
cards and a special place for
a pencil and notebook for
impromptu sketches and notes.

You Will Need

(Seam allowances are included)

- Two 7in x 6in quarter Log cabin patchwork panels (finished size) from:
  - assorted 1in wide light and dark fabric strips
  - two 2½in x 1½in pieces for corner rectangles
- 7in x 1½in beige denim for pocket book spine
- Dark brown cotton pieces:
  - one 16in x 4in for fastener strap
  - one 17in x 4in for wrist strap
  - one 2in x 4in for D-ring loop

- Two 7in x 6in pieces of stiff pelmet interfacing
- Assorted lining fabric pieces:
  - two 7in x 6in (A and G)
  - one 7in x 1¾in (B)
  - one 19in x 2¾in (C)
  - one 7in x 6½in (D)
  - one 7in x 1½in (E)
  - one 12in x 1½in (F)
  - one 7in x 10in (H)
  - one 7in x 9in (I)
- Three 2½in x 2¾in pieces of lightweight iron-on interfacing

- 2in x 42in bias-cut fabric strip
- 1in antique brass D-ring
- 1in antique brass bolt snap
- Antique brass popper fastener and setting tools
- Sewing and quilting threads to tone with patchwork
- Contrasting machine thread
- 2½in diameter circle template
- Assorted A4 and A5 sheets of paper for notebook

Making the Patchwork

1 Begin by making quarter Log Cabin blocks (see Log Cabin, page 102). Each block is made from light and dark 1in strips, with a corner rectangle as shown in **Fig 1**. Sort your fabrics into light and dark tones before machine piecing. Trim the strips to length as you go. The finished width of the strips is ½in. Note, the blocks are mirror images of each other.

Place one completed block on top of one 7in x 6in piece of stiff pelmet interfacing, pin and machine quilt (page 104) in the ditch. There is no need to back the pelmet interfacing.

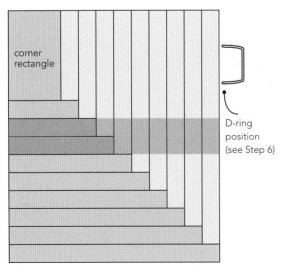
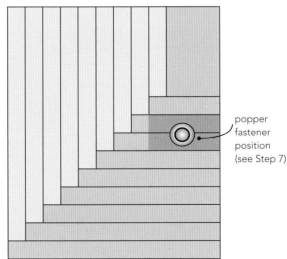

corner rectangle

D-ring position (see Step 6)

popper fastener position (see Step 7)

Fig 1 Quarter Log Cabin patchwork blocks for the outer panels

Constructing the Bag

2 *Making the lining:* Fold fabric strip C as shown in **Fig 2** and press. Iron on the three 2½in x 2¾in pieces of lightweight iron-on interfacing to the wrong side of each pocket front, setting them inside the folds. Machine sew each piece along the fold to stabilize the edge, ¼in from the edge, using a decorative machine stitch if desired. Machine sew fabric piece B to the left side of the pocket strip and D to the right (see **Fig 3**). Fold D to the back so the whole panel measures 7in x 5in and then press. Machine sew along the fold on D to stabilize the edge, ¼in from the edge, as before. Place the completed pocket panel on top of the right side of fabric piece A, line up raw edges at left, top and bottom, and machine sew ⅛in from edge.

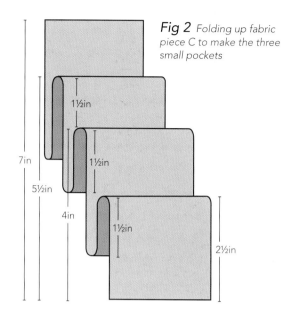

Fig 2 Folding up fabric piece C to make the three small pockets

7in
5½in
4in
1½in
1½in
1½in
2½in

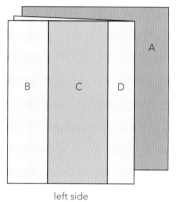

left side

spine

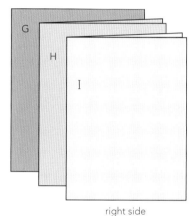

right side

Fig 3 The various fabric pieces making up the pockets and lining

TIP

I USED MACHINE BLANKET STITCH TO STABILIZE THE POCKET EDGES BUT OTHER MACHINE STITCHES ARE SUITABLE, AS LONG AS THEY DON'T STRETCH. IF YOU ARE UNSURE, MAKE A TEST PIECE FIRST. A STRIP OF RIBBON OR FINE BRAID ALSO WORKS WELL.

3 Fold fabric pieces H and I in half to measure 7in x 5in and 7in x 4½in respectively and press. Machine sew each piece along the fold to stabilize the edge, ¼in from the edge, as before. With all pieces right sides up, place H on top of G and I on top of H (see Fig 3), lining up the raw edges at right, top and bottom, and machine sew ⅛in from edge. Machine sew pocket I again to the other layers ½in from top and bottom to make a snug notebook pocket. Fold F in half to measure 6in x 1½in, press and machine sew along the fold, as before. Pin to E to make a pencil pocket. With right sides together, machine sew the left panel and then the right panel to the pencil pocket to complete the lining.

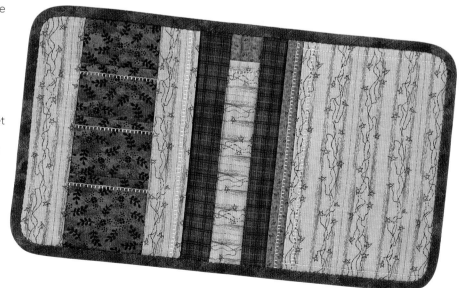

4 *Making straps and loops:* Using the dark brown cotton pieces 16in x 4in, 17in x 4in and 2in x 4in, make the fastener strap, wrist strap and D-ring loop respectively. Following **Fig 4a–d**, fold each piece in half along the length to measure 2in wide and then press. Open this out and fold over each long edge to the centre, using the centre crease as a guide, and fold in half again, so the strip measures 1in wide and press. Putting the fastener strap to one side for the moment, machine sew the wrist strap, sewing one line very close to each long edge and two extra lines ¼in from each edge. Do the same for the D-ring loop. Put the wrist strap aside for Step 7.

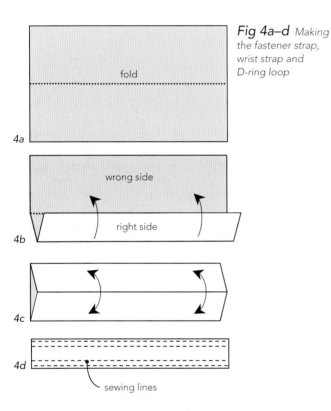

Fig 4a–d *Making the fastener strap, wrist strap and D-ring loop*

4a   fold

4b   wrong side / right side

4c

4d   sewing lines

5 Open out the fastener strap and, at one end, fold under the raw edge by ½in and press, then refold the strap. Start sewing the fastener strap at the raw edge end, stitching around the pressed-in end and continuing to sew along the other edge, as shown in **Fig 5**. Machine sew the first line close to the edge and then sew the second line ¼in from the edge, to make a double row of stitches, as in Step 4. Add the outer part of the popper fastener to the fastener strap, with the centre of the popper ¾in from the end of strap, following the manufacturer's instructions.

Fig 5 *Sewing around the end of the fastener strap*

6 Thread the D-ring on to the fabric loop made in Step 4, fold the loop in half, pin 1in down the side of the back pocket book panel and tack (baste), in the position shown in Fig 1. Now pin the fastener strap to the pocket book back and tack the right end in place. The D-ring loop and the end of the fastener strap will be sewn into the next seam.

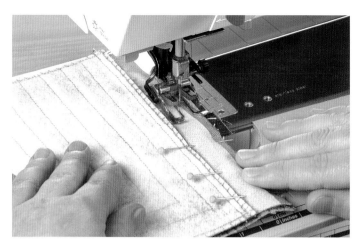

7 With right sides together, pin and machine sew the pocket book back to the 7in x 1½in denim spine strip, then sew the front pocket book panel to the strip. Press towards the spine. The outer panel is now complete. Position and add the inner part of the popper fastener to the pocket book front, with the centre of the popper 1in from the panel edge, as in Fig 1.

8 Using the 2½in circle template, trim each corner of the outer panel and lining to a neat curve. Pin the lining to the outer panel and tack (baste) together. Tack along either side of the spine and, with the outer panel on top, stitch in the ditch along either side of the spine, to hold the lining flat inside. Using the bias-cut strip, make double bias binding (see Making and attaching bindings, page 107). Pin and machine sew the binding around the edge of the pocket book, being careful not to stretch the binding. Start and finish along the bottom edge, so the ends of the bias can be joined smoothly. When the machine stitching is complete, fold the bias binding over and slipstitch it in place all around the bag panel.

9 Now sew the bolt snap to the end of the wrist strap by threading one end of the strap through the loop at the top of the bolt, pinning the raw end of the strap over itself by about 1in. Fold under the other raw end and pin to cover up the end threaded through the bolt. Stitch a figure of eight to secure the strap ends (see Attaching straps and D-rings, page 110). Clip the strap to the D-ring to finish.

IDEA

MAKE A CUSTOMIZED NOTEBOOK BY FOLDING A4 AND A5-SIZED PIECES OF PAPER INSIDE A THIN CARDBOARD A5 COVER. INCLUDE SQUARED OR ISOMETRIC GRAPH PAPER FOR QUICK DESIGN NOTES. USING AN OLD NEEDLE AND A LONG STITCH, MACHINE SEW THE PAGES TOGETHER DOWN THE CENTRE, TYING OFF THE THREAD AT EACH END.

CRAZY PATCHWORK POUCH

This simple drawstring bag has a hidden secret:
it looks authentically Victorian from the outside with
its pretty patches in silks, velvets and prints but the
lining has a zipped pocket for 21st-century essentials.
As a participant at historical festivals, it holds my car
keys and camera while time travelling! The theme can
be changed to suit other periods or brought up to
date with the latest fabrics.

The crazy patchwork on this attractive
pouch is given unity by embellishing
the patches with different embroidery
stitches such as herringbone and
feather stitch in gold-coloured perlé
thread (see the Stitch Library on
page 112). The same thread is also
used to braid the drawstring, the
ends of which are then decorated
with pretty fabric flower buds.

YOU WILL NEED

(Seam allowances are included)

- Two 7¼in x 5½in crazy patchwork panels from various scraps
- One 14¾in length of 1¾in wide decorative ribbon for bag gusset
- Two 8in x 7in muslin pieces for backing patchwork
- One 14¾in x 1¾in piece of calico for backing gusset

- Lining fabric pieces:
  – one 3½in x 5½in
  – one 4¾in x 5½in
  – one 7in x 5½in (for pocket)
  – one 7¼in x 5½in
  – one 14¾in x 1¾in (for gusset)
- 4in zip
- Two 13in lengths of fine cord for drawstring

- Two 3½in squares to match lining fabric for flower bud trims
- Sewing and quilting threads to tone with patchwork
- Cotton perlé thread for hand embroidery

MAKING THE PATCHWORK

1 Begin by making two 7¼in x 5½in pieces of crazy patchwork, using the stitch and flip method (see Crazy Patchwork, page 103). Each piece is made from assorted cotton print, silk and velvet scraps, with oddments of lace and ribbon, stitched to a muslin backing. Cut a paper pattern, shown actual size in **Fig 1**, and mark the outer line on the wrong side of each piece of muslin, centring the pattern on the fabric. Machine sew the crazy patchwork, making sure the patchwork covers the outline. Trim to size when the patchwork is finished and overlock or zigzag the edges. Embellish the seams with various hand embroidery stitches in perlé thread (I used blanket stitch, herringbone stitch, feather stitch and fly stitch – see Stitch Library, page 112). Mark the position of the drawstring channel on the back of each panel, (shown as a pink dashed line in Fig 1) and mark the black dots.

2 Using the 14¾in x 1¾in pieces of ribbon and calico, cut the bag gusset, shown actual size in **Fig 2**. Sew the calico to the back of the ribbon and overlock or zigzag the edges.

CONSTRUCTING THE BAG

TIP

SEW THE GUSSET PANEL AROUND THE CURVED CORNERS WITH THE GUSSET ON TOP – IT'S EASIER!

3 Using one crazy patchwork panel and the completed gusset, pin the gusset to the panel, starting from the bottom centre of the patchwork panel and easing the two pieces together. Match up the end of the gusset stitching line with the two bottom dots in Fig 1. Machine sew together, beginning and ending ¼in from the end of the gusset. Press towards the patchwork panel.

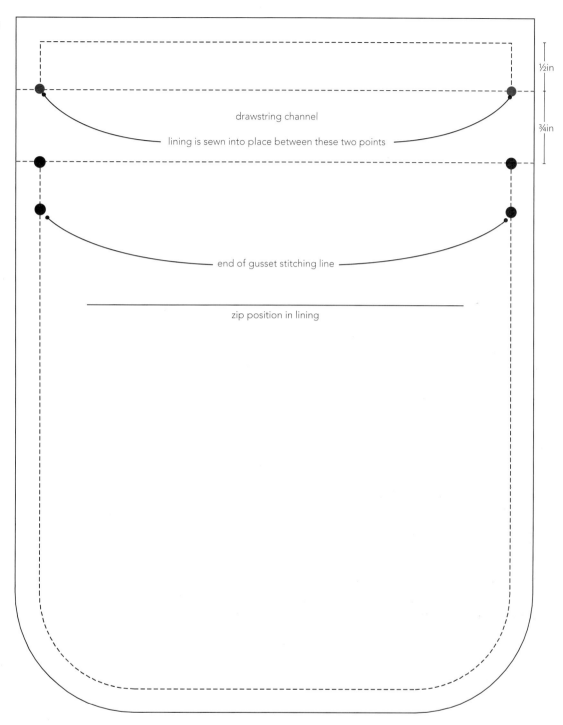

Fig 1 *Pouch pattern (shown actual size)*

½in

¾in

drawstring channel

lining is sewn into place between these two points

end of gusset stitching line

zip position in lining

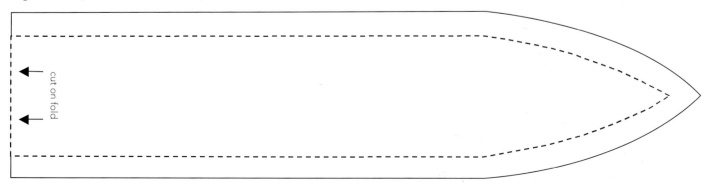

Fig 2 *Gusset pattern (shown actual size)*

cut on fold

CRAZY PATCHWORK POUCH   29

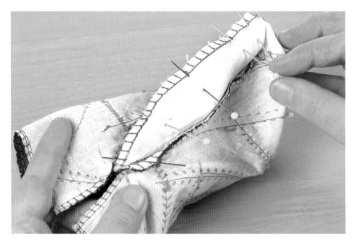

4 Repeat Step 3 with the second patchwork panel, pinning and sewing it to the gusset. When finished, press.

5 Sew the top of the side seam, between the two dots on Fig 1. Turn right side out. The bag outer is now complete.

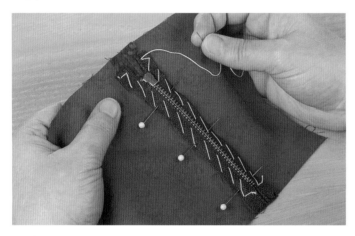

6 *Making the zip pocket and lining:* Cut the curved corners on the bottom of the 4¾in x 5½in lining piece and pin the top to the 3½in x 5½in piece, wrong sides together. Machine sew a ¾in long ½in wide seam at each end of the pinned section. Tack (baste) the central part of the seam and press open. On the wrong side, tack the zip in place (see Inserting zips, page 108).

7 Pin the pocket lining to the back of the zip along the bottom edge as shown and tack (baste) in place.

8 From the right side of the lining, machine sew the zip and pocket lining. Press the pocket fabric towards the bottom of the lining panel.

9 Fold up the pocket fabric, pin it over the top side of the zip then tack (baste) in place. From the right side of the bag, machine sew the zip and pocket lining in place. Remove tacking. Now machine sew the sides of the pocket lining to the sides of the bag panel, ⅛in from the edge – the raw edge of the pocket lining will be caught in the lining assembly seam. Continue to make the lining the same way as the outer bag, but leave a 4in gap unsewn along one side.

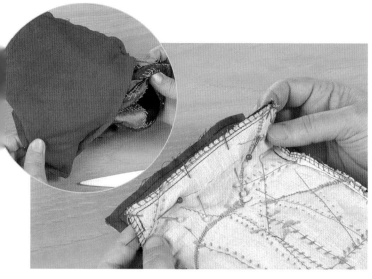

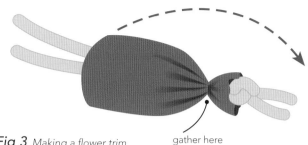

Fig 3 *Making a flower trim*

gather here

10 *Inserting the lining:* Turn the lining right side out and the bag wrong side out. Place the lining inside the bag and pin the lining to the bag's top edge. Machine sew the lining to the bag along either side of the top, starting and finishing at the points shown by red dots in Fig 1, leaving a ¾in gap between the top seam and the side seams for the drawstring channel. Clip the top corners. Bag out, by turning the bag right side out through the lining gap, making sure the top corners are fully turned out. Press the edges around the bag top. Mark and machine stitch the drawstring channel, as shown in Fig 1. Slipstitch the lining gap closed. Insert each drawstring and knot the ends. Stitch through the knot so it can't come undone.

11 *Making the flower trims:* Fold one 3½in square of fabric in half, right sides together, and sew a ¼in seam to make a tube. Press the seam open. Turn half of the tube right side out, so the fabric is double and the seam allowance is hidden. With a double length of sewing cotton, run small running stitches around the raw end of the tube, slip the tube over the knotted end of the first drawstring (with raw ends towards the knot) and gather up tightly, as shown in **Fig 3**. Take a few stitches through the cord and knot to finish off. Fold the tube down over the knot to hide the knot inside.

For optional 'stamens', use yellow perlé or cotton à broder embroidery thread. Pinch the open end of the tube to flatten it and stitch thread through at the creases and leave loose. Pinch the end the other way and stitch another thread through. Hold all four ends of thread and knot together close to the end of the tube. Trim the threads to finish.

IDEA

FOR A SIMPLE VERSION OF THE BAG, LEAVE OUT THE ZIP POCKET. CUT TWO 7¼IN X 5½IN LINING PIECES PLUS A LINING GUSSET AND ASSEMBLE FOLLOWING STEPS 3–5, LEAVING A 4IN GAP UNSEWN.

GLITTER POUCH

The size of the original bag is easily changed for a different look; simply photocopy and enlarge all the pattern pieces by 130% (or more). Here, the stitch and flip crazy patchwork is given an exotic sparkle with scraps of Indian fabrics, shot silks and irresistible glittery trims (see *Mail-Order Suppliers,* page 118). To simplify the design, I left out the zip pocket from the lining. Bridal fabrics and lace could also be used for a romantic look in ivory and cream.

PUDDING BAG

The original 'pudding' bag was adopted from a friend's grandmother, who stored her fabric scraps in an old sheet, with the corners tied like an old-fashioned suet pudding. Playing with the pudding fuelled my passion for fabric. My updated version is a 44in diameter circle of crazy patchwork, gathered up by a drawstring through chunky eyelets. It has a stripy bias binding edge to match the lining.

The pudding bag will entertain all fabric addicts and is a great way to get your scrap collection under control. It is easily opened by untying the drawstring, which has unusual brass 'bell' ends – actually light pulls from a hardware store.

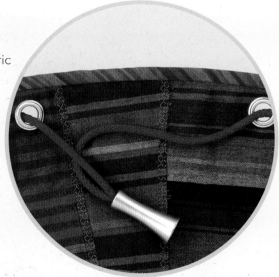

You Will Need

(Seam allowances are included)

- One 44in diameter circular foundation pieced crazy patchwork panel from striped and checked cotton fabric scraps, 2in x 3in minimum size
- One 44in diameter circle of backing fabric
- One 46in square of lining fabric
- 1¾in x 146in bias-cut strip, for double bias binding (see page 107)
- Twenty-four large brass eyelets and appropriate setting tools
- Two 74in lengths of medium-weight nylon cord for drawstrings
- Two decorative 'bell' ends for drawstrings
- Sewing and quilting threads to tone with patchwork

MAKING THE PATCHWORK

IDEA

Using the same thread and stitch for all the appliqué gives greater unity to a variety of different fabrics but you could try shading from light to dark or from one colour to another. Or just use up as many different thread oddments as possible!

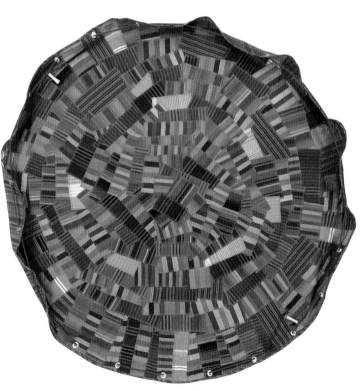

1 Begin by making a circular piece of crazy patchwork for the bag outer. Cut out a 44in diameter circle from the backing fabric and machine sew around it, ⅛in from the edge, to stabilize the bias-cut parts of the edge. Select a decorative or utility machine stitch suitable for edging the appliqué shapes. Begin the crazy patchwork (see page 103) at the outer edge, appliquéing randomly sized rectangles and wedge shapes all around the edge, overlapping the previous shape with each new one. Allow the strips to overlap the outer edge, trimming the edge to line up with the circular backing when the appliqué is finished. When the outer edge is complete, continue adding more appliqué, spiralling in towards the centre. I changed the direction of the appliqué pieces after the first round, so most of the stripes run outwards. The picture (right) shows the outside of the finished bag, revealing this change in stripe direction.

Constructing the Bag

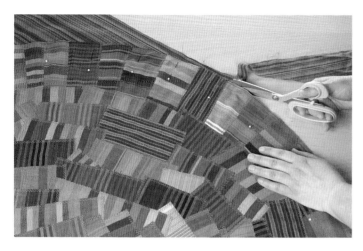

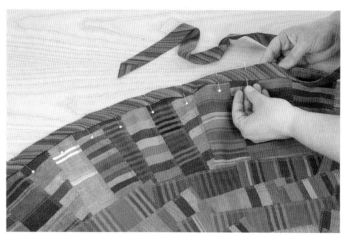

2 With the patchwork panel and the square of lining wrong sides together, pin and machine sew together around the edge, stitching ⅛in from the edge. Trim the lining to match the patchwork.

3 Using the bias-cut strip, make double bias binding (see Making and attaching bindings page 107). Pin and machine sew the binding around the edge of the circle, being careful not to stretch the binding. Join the ends on a 45-degree angle as shown on page 107. When the machine stitching is complete, fold the bias binding over and slipstitch (hem stitch) it in place around the edge of the bag.

(see Making and attaching bindings page 107) ... as shown on page 107.

TIP

USING A STRIPED
FABRIC FOR YOUR
BIAS BINDING GIVES A
LOVELY SPINNING EFFECT,
ESPECIALLY ON
A CURVED EDGE!

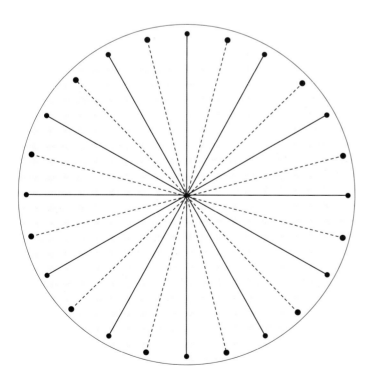

Fig 1 Insert eyelets at twelve equal intervals, like a clock face, as shown by the dots at the end of the solid lines; then insert another twelve between the first set, as shown by the dots at the end of the dashed lines

4 Mark the position of the 24 eyelets as shown in **Fig 1**, positioning them approximately ¾in from the bound edge. Following the manufacturer's instructions and using the appropriate setting tools, punch holes and set the first twelve eyelets. Position and set the remaining twelve. Thread one drawstring cord through twelve eyelets and the second cord through the other twelve, and then thread one end of both cords through the first decorative bell and knot. Repeat this with the other two ends to finish your bag.

LEAFY SATCHEL

This pretty satchel can be worn as a shoulder bag – great for a walk or an outdoor party – or as a satchel when cycling in the countryside. The lining has a zip pocket to keep keys, small change or extra memory cards for your digital camera safe. It's also the perfect project for practising raw-edge appliqué and free-motion machine quilting. The simple shape is quick to make and can easily be varied (see page 41).

The top of this bag features a tough linen double diamond-shaped appliqué with raw edges, where it will be handled the most. Easy strip patchwork is decorated with leaves stamped on plain fabric, cut out and sewn on as raw-edge appliqué.

YOU WILL NEED

(Unless otherwise stated, add seam allowances to fabric and wadding sizes – see page 5)

- One 17in x 6in patchwork panel from assorted 1in and 2in strips
- Oddments of bright green cotton for leaves
- Leaf pattern rubber stamp
- Fabric ink stamp pads in red and black
- One 5in square of linen
- One 5in square of two-tone shot silk dupion or similar
- One 18in x 7in piece of backing fabric

- 2oz cotton wadding (batting) pieces:
  - one 18in x 7in for bag
  - one 47in x 1in for strap
- Lining fabric pieces (seam allowances included):
  - one 10¾in x 6½in
  - one 7¼in x 6½in
  - one 9in x 6½in for pocket lining
- 4in zip
- One button of your choice
- One 3½in x 1in strip for button loop (includes seam allowance)
- One 50in x 2¼in fabric strip for strap

- Two 3in x 2in fabric pieces for D-ring loops
- 1in wide webbing:
  - one 50in length for strap
  - two 3in lengths for D-ring loops
- Two 1in antique nickel D-rings
- Two 1¼in antique nickel bolt snaps
- Sewing and quilting threads to tone with patchwork
- Shaded machine embroidery thread
- Machine embroidery needle
- 2½in diameter circle template

MAKING THE PATCHWORK

1 Make one 5in x 6in and one 11in x 6in patchwork panel from assorted strips, finished width 1in (see Patchwork Techniques page 97). Machine sew the strips into two pieces, including some strips made by sewing together shorter pieces. Machine sew each piece to either side of a 6½in x 2½in strip (includes seam allowance) – see **Fig 1**. Press towards the strip. With the wadding (batting) and backing, make a quilt sandwich (see page 104) and then machine quilt. Quilt the strips in the ditch, then free-motion quilt the 2in strip with leaf shapes.

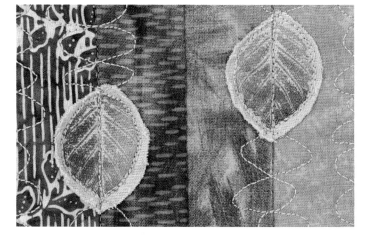

2 Print leaf shapes using oddments of bright green cotton, a leaf pattern rubber stamp and fabric ink stamp pads in red and black. Make sure the fabric is free from starch or other finishes and follow the manufacturer's instructions to set the ink colours. Print shaded leaves by inking up part of the stamp with red and part with black. When the prints are dry, cut out the shapes, about ⅛in larger all round and arrange as you wish. Pin the leaves to the bag panel and machine sew in place while quilting free-motion wavy lines up and down the strips.

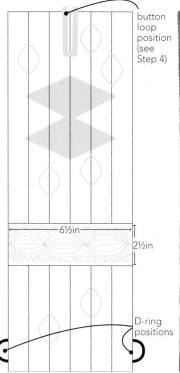

button loop position (see Step 4)

6½in

2½in

D-ring positions

Fig 1
Patchwork layout showing strips and position of appliqué shapes

IDEA

ADD AS MANY LEAVES AS YOU LIKE: THE POSITIONS OF MINE ARE SHOWN IN FIG 1. INCLUDE OTHER LEAF SHAPES IF YOU HAVE A VARIETY OF PRINTING STAMPS AVAILABLE.

3 To make the double diamond-shaped appliqué, quarter fold the linen and silk squares together – fold in half and in half again until you have a folded 2½in square. Cut freehand along the dotted lines shown in **Fig 2** – practise first with a piece of paper! When the fabric is unfolded you should have two linked diamond shapes in each fabric. Pin the shape to the top of the bag, as shown by the shaded area in Fig 1, with the linen on top. Quilt spirals in straight lines in shaded thread, starting at the outside about ½in from the raw edge and working inwards, working with the machine feed dogs up. Rub over the raw bias edges to fray them. The bag panel now is complete.

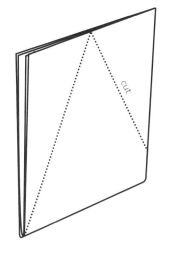

Fig 2 Folding the linen and silk into quarters ready to cut the double diamond shape

CONSTRUCTING THE BAG

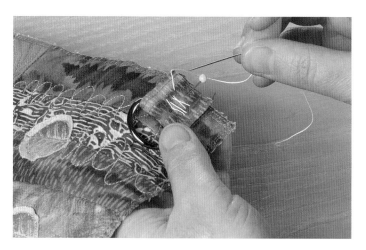

4 ***Attaching the D-rings:*** Using the two 3in x 2in fabric pieces and 3in lengths of webbing, make fabric loops for the D-rings. Fold each fabric piece in half along the length to measure 1in wide and press. Open this out and fold each long edge over to the centre, using the centre pressed crease as a guide, so the strip measures 1in wide, and then press. Pin and machine sew one piece of webbing to each fabric piece, covering the raw fabric edges with the webbing. Machine sew two rows close to the webbing edge and two rows ¼in from the edge. Thread a D-ring on to one completed loop and fold the loop so the webbing is inside. Pin to the bag panel, 1in from inside edge, as shown in Fig 1 by the two black D-shapes, and tack (baste) as shown.

5 Now sew the side seams. With right sides together, fold up the front of the bag (bottom of Fig 1), so that the 2in base strip is folded exactly in half. Pin and stitch the side seams, starting ¼in from the inside edge, as shown.

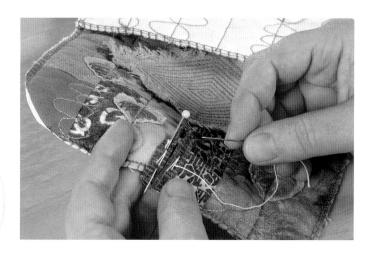

6 Using the 3½in x 1in strip and following the folding diagrams for the Quilter's Pocket Book (page 24), make the button loop. Machine sew along the loop twice, close to the edge. Fold the loop in half and tack (baste) the loop to the centre of the flap part of the bag panel, as shown by the green loop in Fig 1. Remember to check that the button can go through the loop easily.

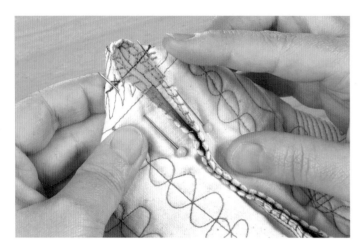

7 With the bag wrong side out, fold a bottom corner point to form a right angle, with the side seam running into the point in the centre. Mark a line at right angles to the side seam, ½in from the point, then pin and machine sew across. Trim off the small triangular flap of fabric. Repeat for the other corner.

8 *Making and inserting the lining:* Using the three pieces of lining fabric and the 4in zip, make a zipped pocket following Steps 6–9 on page 30. Now assemble the lining in the same way as the bag outer, remembering to leave a 3½in gap in one side seam.

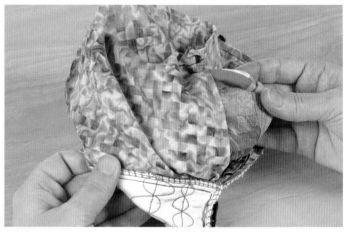

9 With the bag inside out and the lining right side out, place the lining inside the bag. Line up and pin the bag flap. Using the 2½in circle template, mark and trim the flap corners into neat curves. Pin across the top of the bag and stitch, beginning and ending the stitching at the side seams between the red pins, as shown above. Then stitch from side seam to side seam around the bag flap.

10 Clip the corners where the flap meets the bag top. Bag out, by turning the bag right side out through the lining gap, making sure the top of the flap is fully turned out. Press the edges all round and topstitch around the bag flap and top, stitching ⅛in from the edge. Slipstitch the lining gap closed. Hand sew a button to the bottom centre of the bag front, taking care not to stitch through the lining.

11 *Making the strap:* Following the instructions for the D-ring loops in Step 4, make a longer length for the bag strap. After pressing the fabric, open up the fold and place the 47in x 1in strip of wadding (batting) inside, then refold, pin the webbing in place and stitch. Note that the wadding is cut shorter than the length of the strip so 1½in at each end has no wadding inside. Thread one end through a bolt snap, fold the raw edge over and stitch in a figure of eight (see Attaching straps and D-rings, page 110). Repeat for the other end. Clip the strap to the finished bag.

TIP

LONG THIN STRIPS OF WADDING (BATTING) ARE USUALLY LEFT OVER WHEN A LARGE QUILT IS TRIMMED. IF YOU DON'T HAVE A LONG LENGTH, SHORTER PIECES CAN BE BUTTED TOGETHER TO FILL THE STRAP.

Party Party

Retro styling in black, white and bright pink makes this version of the bag distinctive and chic. The elongated star blocks (see the Four-Patch Star in the Block Library page 116), each rectangle 2½in x 1½in, were free-motion machine quilted with twirly loops and flowers in pink thread. See page 31 for making the flower trims. No longer really a satchel, carry it clutch style or loop a strap around the single D-ring, and party!

LUSCIOUS BERRY BAG

Almost good enough to eat with their blend of fruity colours, these festive little berry bags are perfect for gifts or just for fun. I delved in my scrap bag to make a rectangle of crazy patchwork, cutting four identically shaped panels to create the bag. The patchwork is embellished with machine stitching and each section topped with a fabric leaf.

The 'leaves' on this bag are created from two pieces of co-ordinating batik fabric, while the drawstrings, which run through a channel around the top, feature plump bobbles in the darker batik fabric.

You Will Need

(For one bag – all pieces include seam allowances)

- One 9in x 8½in piece of crazy patchwork from fabric scraps – cotton prints, silks, ribbons and velvets
- One 9in x 8½in piece of calico for backing patchwork

- Batik fabric pieces:
  – one 9in x 8½in for lining
  – two 1¾in x 5½in for the drawstring channel
  – two 6in x 3½in for leaves
  – two 3in diameter circles for stuffed bobble trims

- Stuffing for bobble trims
- Two 15in lengths of fine cord for drawstring
- Sewing and quilting threads to tone with patchwork
- Decorative machine embroidery threads

Making the Patchwork

Idea

IMITATE NATURE BY USING TWO CO-ORDINATING BATIKS FOR THE LEAVES, SO THE UNDERSIDE HAS A LIGHTER OR DARKER COLOUR THAN THE TOP.

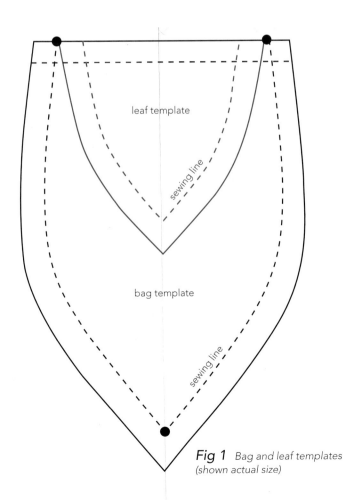

1 Begin by making one 9in x 8½in piece of crazy patchwork, using the raw-edge appliqué method (see Crazy Patchwork, page 103). The piece is made from assorted scraps stitched to a calico backing. Overlap the pieces slightly and use machine stitches, such as blanket stitch and various overlocking stitches in an assortment of toning threads to hold the raw edges in place. Machine sew some extra zigzag lines over the completed piece.

2 Cut paper or cardboard templates, shown actual size in **Fig 1**, and use the larger one to cut out four berry panels from your crazy patchwork piece, arranging the outlines on the patchwork as shown in **Fig 2**. Mark the dots shown on the diagram on the back of the berry panels.

leaf template

sewing line

bag template

sewing line

Fig 1 *Bag and leaf templates (shown actual size)*

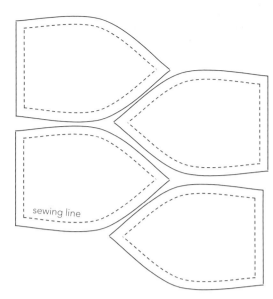

Fig 2 Layout for cutting one
set of bag panels from crazy
patchwork (not to scale)

sewing line

◻ CONSTRUCTING THE BAG

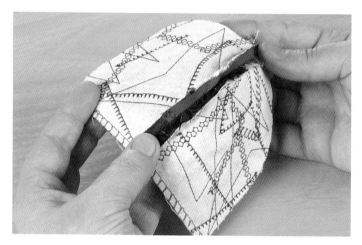

3 *Making the berry:* Place two berry panels right sides together, pin and machine sew along one curved side between the dots, beginning and ending ¼in from the end of the piece. Press the seam open. Repeat for the remaining two berry panels. The bag is now in two halves.

4 Place one half of the bag, right side out, inside the other half, which should be inside out. Line up the previous seams where they meet at the bottom. Pin and machine sew the two halves together, between the dots. Press the seam open. The bag outer is now complete.

TIP

WHEN PRESSING
THE BAG SEAMS, USE THE
END OF A NARROW SLEEVE
IRONING BOARD OR A SHAPED
TAILOR'S HAM TO HELP HOLD
THE CURVED SEAM OPEN. YOU
CAN IMPROVISE WITH THE
END OF A ROLLED UP
HAND TOWEL.

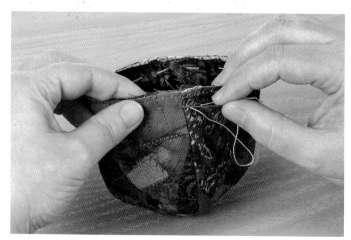

5 Using the 9in x 8½in lining fabric, repeat Steps 3 and 4 to make the lining. With the bag right side out and the lining inside out, place the lining inside the bag, pin and tack (baste) ⅜in from the top of the bag.

6 *Making the leaves:* Using two 6in x 3½in fabric pieces (for leaves) and the leaf template from Fig 1, cut out four leaf pieces from each fabric, arranging the outlines as shown in **Fig 3**. Pin one piece of each fabric right sides together and machine sew, as indicated by the dashed line. Clip the point, turn right sides out, push out the points and press. Machine sew a leaf 'vein' down the centre from the top raw edge of the leaf, stopping ½in from the end and then turning and sewing back to the top. Repeat for the other three leaves.

7 Line up the stitched 'vein' of the first leaf with one of the berry seams, and the top of the leaf with the top of the bag, and pin. Continue pinning leaves around the top.

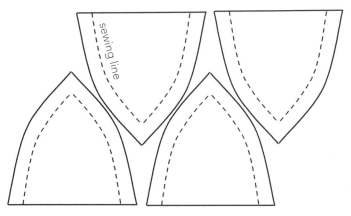

sewing line

Fig 3 *Layout for cutting one set of leaves from fabric (not to scale)*

8 *Making the drawstring channel:* On the wrong side, fold under ⅜in at the ends of each of the 1¾in x 5½in pieces and press. With the right side of the channel piece against the outside of the berry and leaves, pin the end to line up with the centre of one leaf, skip the next leaf and line up the other end with the centre of the leaf on the opposite side of the bag. The long edge of the channel will line up with the top of the bag. Ease the channel piece to the bag and tack (baste). Repeat with other piece. Sewing from the inside, machine sew the channel, leaves and berry together and then zigzag the raw edge.

TIP

TINY WASTE SCRAPS OF POLYESTER WADDING (BATTING) ARE GOOD FOR STUFFING BOBBLES!

9 Press the seam towards the drawstring channel, fold under a ¼in hem and fold the channel to the inside of the bag. Hand sew the hem in place (see Hemming stitch, page 113). Insert each drawstring cord, knot the ends and stitch through the knot so it can't come undone.

10 Hand sew a gathering thread around the edge of one 3in diameter circle, folding under the edge a scant ¼in as you go. Gather the circle slightly, stuff it and push the knotted end of the cord inside. Continue to gather the circle tightly and take several stitches through the cord and gathered edge before fastening off the thread. Repeat for the second bobble.

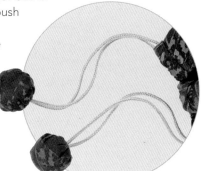

Spooky Hallowe'en

Made mostly from batiks, this Hallowe'en pumpkin is great for trick or treating, whether you are giving or collecting the treats. The berry bag pattern was enlarged by 220% on a photocopier and assembled without the leaf trim. The face was machine appliquéd, with zigzagged edges. Create mini tassels by fraying the ends of the drawstring cord. Stick to washable fabrics and wadding (batting), so you can remove chocolate and candy goo!

Log Cabin Saddlebag

Four pockets hidden under this bag's flaps give ample room for all you need, including books and magazines. It is easier to make than it looks, with two flat layers, sewn together across the centre top. Sepia and taupe country prints contrast with the Log Cabin blocks on the outer flaps, which conceal zipped pockets. Use a feature fabric for the block centres or print your own photos on the computer, as I've done (see Step 2). My 'Victorian' photos were taken at a local festival. The saddlebag co-ordinates with the bags on pages 20, 73 and 89.

The atmospheric photographs are also on the back of the bag. The photos were printed directly on to ready-to-use fabric sheets, pre-treated to create permanent images with all injet printers (see Mail-Order Suppliers, page 118). The paper backing was removed before ironing to set the image and the fabric rinsed to remove excess ink.

YOU WILL NEED

(Unless otherwise stated, add seam allowances to fabric and wadding sizes – see page 5)

- Two 12in square patchwork panels from four 6in blocks:
  – four Log Cabin blocks with dark shades dominant
  – four Log Cabin blocks with light shades dominant
- A4 fabric sheet for computer printing
- Two 9in x 12½in strip patchwork panels (seam allowances included) from forty-eight 9in x 1in strips
- Brown cotton fabric pieces (seam allowances included):
  – one 27in x 12½in for inner panel front
  – one 2½in x 12½in for centre top panel

- two 12½in x 12½in for lining zipped pockets
- two 9in x 12½in for lining inner pockets
- two 2in x 12½in strips for binding inner pocket tops
- two 2in x 84in bias-cut fabric strips for binding
- Beige denim pieces (seam allowances included):
  – one 27in x 12½in for inner panel back
  – one 2½in x 12½in for backing centre top panel
  – one 41½in x 2½in for strap
  – two 2½in x 12½in for top of zipped pockets
  – two 11in x 12½in for bottom of zipped pockets

- Backing fabric pieces:
  – two 13in squares for Log Cabin panels
  – two 10in x 13in for strip patchwork panels
- 2oz cotton wadding (batting):
  – two 13in squares for Log Cabin panels
  – two 10in x 13in for strip patchwork panels
- Heavyweight 1in webbing:
  – one 41½in length for strap
  – two 3in lengths for D-ring loops
- Two 1in antique brass D-rings
- Two 1¼in antique brass bolt snaps
- Two 12in zips
- Sewing and quilting threads to tone with patchwork
- 2½in diameter circle template

MAKING THE PATCHWORK

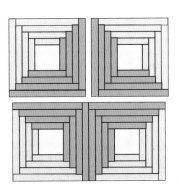

Fig 2 *Layout of the four Log Cabin blocks*

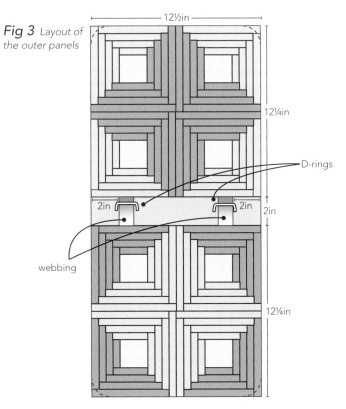

Fig 3 *Layout of the outer panels*

12½in

12¼in

D-rings

2in 2in 2in

webbing

12¼in

1 Begin by making eight 6in Log Cabin blocks (see page 102). Each block is machine sewn from an assortment of light and dark 1in strips plus one 2½in centre square (see Cutting fabric strips page 98). All the blocks are constructed identically as in **Fig 1** (opposite page) but the dark/light placement on one panel is the opposite of the other – the first strips sewn to the centre square in each Log Cabin block are light on one panel (bag front), dark on the other (bag back), and the patchwork continues this sequence (see **Fig 2**).

2 To create the feature fabric for the block centres, use the computer programme of your choice to arrange your selection of photographs on one page, making sure you will be able to cut 2½in squares – make a test print on paper first. Following the manufacturer's instructions, print and set the images on the fabric (see also the Tip, right). Cut the central squares and piece the Log Cabin blocks, making sure the photos will be the right way up when the blocks are sewn together in panels in groups of four, as shown in **Fig 3**.

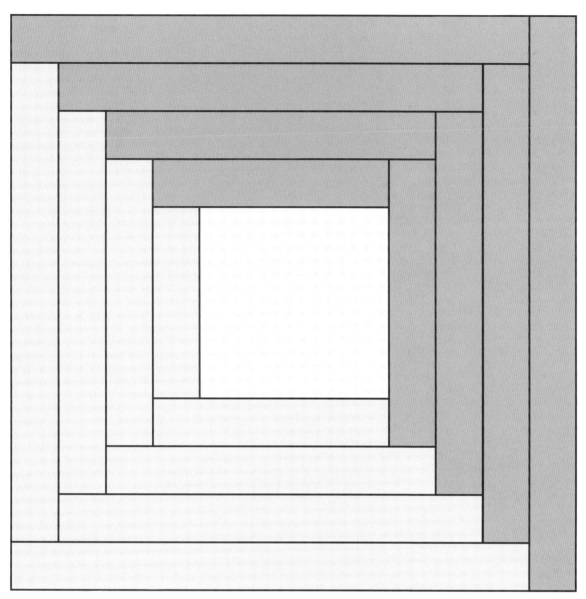

Fig 1 *Single Log Cabin block (shown actual size)*

TIP

PRINT PRE-TREATED FABRICS, AND FABRICS DIPPED IN SETTING FLUID, DIRECTLY FROM YOUR HOME COMPUTER. SOME PHOTO TRANSFERS CAN BE ALSO MADE WITH PHOTOCOPIERS.

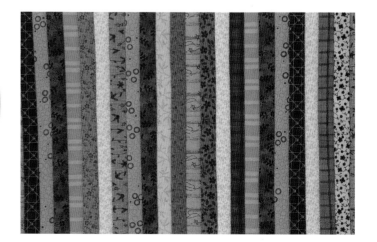

3 With one panel, wadding (batting) and backing, make a quilt sandwich (see page 104) and then machine quilt (page 104). Quilt in the ditch horizontally and vertically across the centre of the block, then quilt in the ditch in a spiral from the centre of each Log Cabin block outwards. Quilt the other panel in the same way.

4 Now make a strip patchwork panel from twenty-four 9in x 1in strips. With the wadding (batting) and backing, make a quilt sandwich (see page 104) and then machine quilt along each strip in the ditch.

5 *Making the inner pockets:* Pin and sew one 9in x 12½in piece of lining to the back of each strip patchwork panel, wrong sides together, and overlock or zigzag the edges. Using the 2in x 12½in strip, make double straight binding (see page 107). Pin and machine sew one binding strip to the top front of each strip patchwork pocket. Then fold the binding over and slipstitch it in place along the back of the pocket top.

6 Shape the middle of the 27in x 12½in piece of denim for the inner panel back, as shown in **Fig 4**. Fold in half along the centre line to cut an identical slight curve into the middle, so the centre is ½in narrower on each side than the ends. The curve begins 9½in from each end. Use the first curve as a guide to cutting the second one, by folding the panel in half along its length. Use the shaped panel as a pattern to cut the 27in x 12½in piece of brown cotton to size, pinning them wrong sides together. Machine sew and overlock or zigzag both pieces together. Pin the pockets made in Step 5 to each end. Use the 2½in circle template to trim the corners to a neat curve. Machine sew the pockets to the panel, ⅛in from the edge. The inner layer panel is now complete.

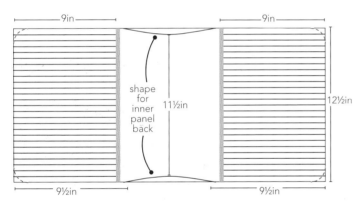

Fig 4 *Layout of inner pockets, with denim shaping*

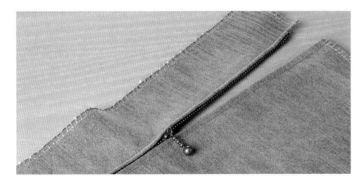

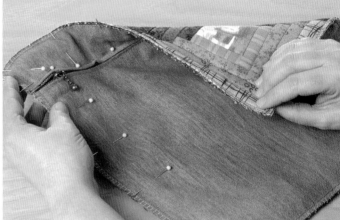

7 *Making the zipped pockets:* Using one 2½in x 12½in top piece, one 11in x 12½in bottom piece and one 12in zip, insert the zip to open on the right, as shown. Tack (baste) the two pieces right sides together ½in from the edge and press open. On the wrong side, tack the zip in place and machine sew (see Inserting a zip invisibly, page 108). Repeat for the second panel, with the zip opening to the left.

8 Complete the zipped pocket panels by pinning one Log Cabin panel to one 12½in x 12½in lining piece, wrong sides together, and machine sew all round. Pin the first zipped pocket panel (completed in Step 7) to the back of the Log Cabin panel with the light cross design in the centre (bag back). The wrong side of the zipped panel will be against the right side of the panel lining and the zip closer to the top of the panel. Make sure the Log Cabin centre pictures are the right way up! Use the 2½in circle template to trim the bottom corners to a neat curve. Machine sew the pockets to the panel, ⅛in from the edge and overlock the edge. Repeat for the second Log Cabin panel.

9 *Assembling the centre top panel:* Pin the 2½in x 12½in denim and cotton pieces wrong sides together and then machine sew all round, ⅛in from the edge. Thread one D-ring on to the 3in length of webbing, pin each end to the edges of the centre top panel, 2in from the side, as shown in Fig 3. Tack (baste) and machine sew. Repeat with the second D-ring. Note that the webbing is longer than the width of the panel, so the D-ring can move freely.

10 With the zipped pocket panels completed in Step 7, pin one pocket panel right sides together to the centre top panel and machine sew as shown. Repeat with the second pocket panel. Press the seam towards the centre top panel. The outer layer panel is now complete.

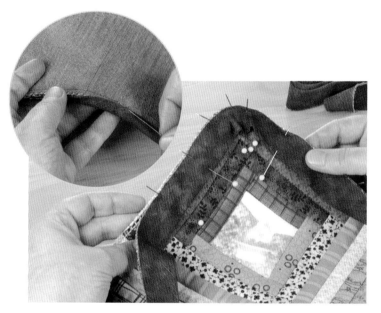

11 Using the bias-cut strips, make double bias binding (see Making and attaching bindings, page 107). Pin and machine sew the binding around the edge of each panel, being careful not to stretch the binding. Start and finish along a straight edge, so the ends of the bias can be joined smoothly. When the machine stitching is complete, fold the bias binding over and hem stitch it in place all around the bag panel.

12 Complete the bag by placing the inner layer panel right side up and the outer layer panel centred on top. Pin, tack (baste) and then machine sew the two panels together, stitching in the ditch along either side of the centre top panel.

13 *Making the strap:* With the 41½in x 2½in denim piece, the webbing and two bolt snaps, make a strap following the method shown for the Leafy Satchel on page 40, omitting the wadding (batting) strip. Clip the strap to the bag to finish.

IDEA

You could make a second, shorter strap
to carry the bag briefcase-style.

SECRET POCKET SACK

This versatile bag can be a rucksack (right) or shoulder bag (below), depending on how you clip the adjustable straps in place. The secret zipped pocket is hidden in the curved flap, accessible by unhooking the decorative clasp. Gorgeous oriental fabrics are perfect as a large-scale feature fabric, while the off-centre Log Cabin clamshell patchwork uses smaller patterns and stripes. Appliqué circles and big stitch quilting add detail.

The secret pocket sack is easily changed from a rucksack to this handy shoulder bag by clipping both straps through both D-rings. A drawstring gives easy access to the large main section, while the flower buds on the drawstrings are a pretty finishing touch.

YOU WILL NEED

(Seam allowancces are included)

- Eight 6in square (finished size) off-centre Log Cabin blocks from 1in and 1½in strips from six different fabrics
- Four 14½in x 1½in strips for vertical sashing, to match Log Cabin fabrics
- Four 6½in x 1½in strips for horizontal sashing, to match front and back 'clamshell'
- Three 3in diameter plain cotton circles for appliqué
- Three 2½in diameter printed cotton circles for appliqué
- Two 3½in cotton squares, for flower bud trims

- Feature fabric pieces for pocket:
  – two 8½in x 12in
  – two 3½in x 1in for ends of zip
- Striped cotton fabric pieces:
  – one 31in x 3½in for drawstring channel
  – two 52in x 3in for bag straps
  – two 2in x 3in for D-ring loops
- Calico backing fabric pieces:
  – two 8½in x 12in for pocket section
  – one 15in x 14in for front section
  – one 15in x 16in for back section
- 2oz cotton wadding (batting) pieces:
  – one 15in x 14in for front section
  – one 15in x 16in for back section
- Lining fabric pieces:

  – two 8½in x 12in for pocket
  – one 14in x 13in for front section
  – one 14in x 15in for back section
- One 8in zip
- One 48in length of medium-weight cord for drawstring
- Two ¾in antique brass slide adjusters
- Two ¾in antique brass snaps
- Two ¾in antique brass D-rings
- One antique brass two-part decorative hook fastener
- Sewing and quilting threads to tone with patchwork
- Shaded cotton perlé No.8 or similar for big stitch quilting

MAKING THE PATCHWORK

1 Begin by making eight 6in square off-centre Log Cabin blocks (see Log Cabin page 102). The blocks were machine sewn without a foundation using the walking foot and the strips trimmed to length as they were sewn. Note the placement of the different fabrics and the varying strip widths, shown in **Fig 1** (front panel) and **Fig 2** (back panel). Once the blocks are completed, assemble the front and back panels using sashing strips.

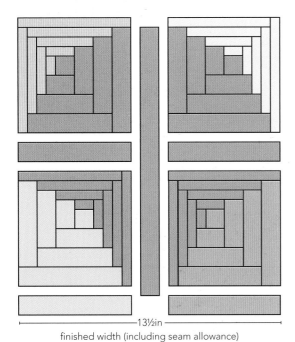

─13½in─
finished width (including seam allowance)

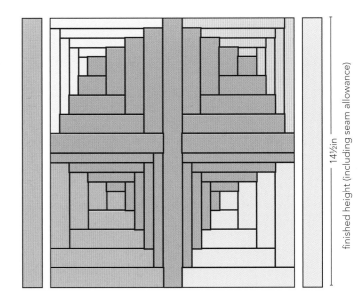

14½in
finished height (including seam allowance)

Fig 1 Panel for the front of the bag, made up of four off-centre Log Cabin blocks with sashing strips added as shown

Fig 2 Panel for the back of the bag, made up of four off-centre Log Cabin blocks with sashing strips added as shown

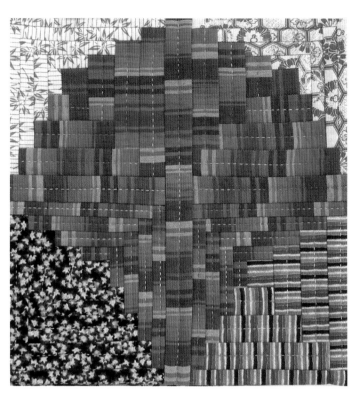

2 With the back panel, wadding (batting) and backing, make a quilt sandwich (see page 104) and then machine quilt (page 104). Quilt in the ditch horizontally and vertically across the centre of the block, then quilt in the ditch in a spiral from the centre of each Log Cabin block outwards. Repeat for the front panel.

IDEA

THE CIRCULAR APPLIQUE DETAILS ON THIS BAG ARE THE PERFECT OPPORTUNITY TO USE A DIRECTIONAL FEATURE FABRIC, SUCH AS A LANDSCAPE OR FIGURE DESIGN.

3 Appliqué three circle motifs to the front panel (see Appliqué page 103), arranged as shown in the picture, left: appliqué the plain circle first, then appliqué the printed circle on top. An easy way to hem on circular appliqués is to cut a thin cardboard circle ½in smaller than the appliqué circle fabric, sew running stitch ⅛in from the edge around the circle, gather up the circle over the cardboard template and press the 'hem' in place. Once the fabric has cooled and the crease is set, remove the card, tack the circle to the background fabric and appliqué. Using the shaded perlé thread, hand quilt big stitch (see page 106) along the centre of each patchwork strip. Quilt around each appliqué circle with whipped running stitch (see Stitch Library page 113 and the Tip, below).

TIP
TEXTURED EMBROIDERY THREADS, FINE METALLIC THREAD OR VERY FINE SILK RIBBON ARE ALL SUITABLE FOR WHIPPED RUNNING STITCH, AS THEY ARE PULLED THROUGH THE FABRIC ONLY AT THE START AND FINISH.

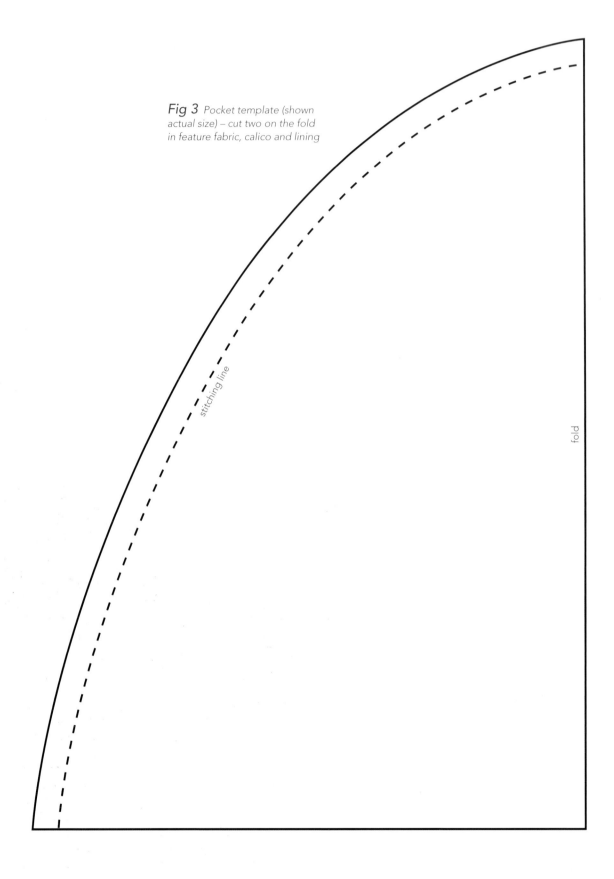

Fig 3 *Pocket template (shown actual size) – cut two on the fold in feature fabric, calico and lining*

stitching line

fold

CONSTRUCTING THE BAG

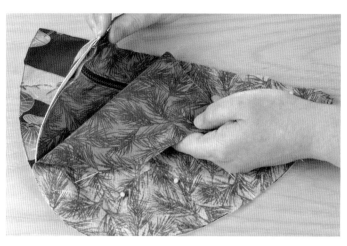

4 *Making the pocket:* Cut out the pocket panels in feature fabric using the actual size template in **Fig 3** opposite. Cut a 2in wide strip parallel to the straight edge of one panel only. Cut the pocket lining and backing fabrics to match the feature fabric pieces. Sew the calico backing fabric pieces to the back of the feature fabric pieces, ⅛in from the edge. Insert the zip into the pocket following the same method given for the Tringle Bag (Step 4, page 71): start by folding and sewing one 3½in x 1in piece to each end of the zip, and then sew the zip into the lining and feature fabrics in one, as shown.

5 Layer the pocket pieces with the pocket front (the piece without the zip) face up, with the zipped section face down and the remaining piece of the lining face down. Now pin around the curved edge and machine sew the layers together with a ¼in seam.

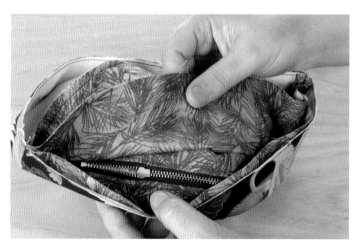

6 Carefully clip the seam allowance around the curve – do not clip right up to the seam, ⅛in is fine. Turn the pocket right sides out, as shown, and press around the curve.

IDEA

THE POCKET PANELS WOULD LOOK GOOD IN AN ORIENTAL BROCADE OR WITH METALLIC THREAD AND BEAD EMBELLISHMENTS.

7 *Making the straps and loops:* Using two striped cotton pieces 52in x 3in and two 2in x 3in, make the straps and D-ring loops respectively, as described for the Quilters' Pocket Book (Step 4, page 24). Machine sew each strap, sewing one line very close to each long edge. Thread one D-ring on to a short completed loop, fold the loop in half, pin to the side of the back panel, 1in up from the panel base, and tack (baste) as shown. Thread one slide adjuster on to one long strap, slide it to the centre, thread both halves of the strap through the loop on the snap and back through the slide adjuster. Pin and tack the ends of the long strap to the top edge of the back panel, 2¾in from the centre of the back panel and placing the strap ends side by side, as shown.

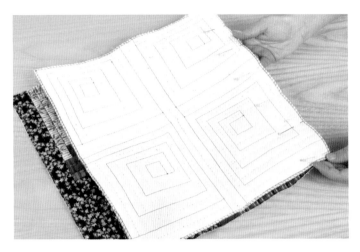

8 *Assembling the main bag section:* With right sides together, pin and sew the back and front bag panels together along the side seams only. Repeat for the bag lining. Press seams to one side and then turn the bag outer right side out.

9 With the zip side of the pocket and the front of the bag right sides together, pin the pocket and bag front together along the bottom edge and tack (baste). Now turn the bag inside out.

TIP

IF YOU HAVE USED HEAVIER FABRICS, SEW THE BAG BASE AND THE LINING BASE SEAMS SEPARATELY.

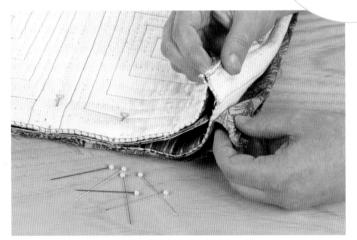

10 *Sewing the lining and pocket into the bag:* With the bag and the lining inside out and the side seams lining up, line up the bottom edges, and then pin and sew across the bag base. This attaches the pocket to the bag and sews in the lining with just one seam.

11 Get hold of the bag pocket and gently turn the bag right side out. Make sure the bottom corners are fully turned out. Sew the hook part of the decorative clip to the top of the pocket curve, being careful not to stitch right through to the other side of the pocket. Fold the pocket up and place and stitch the loop part of the clip to the front of the bag. Line up the top edges of the lining and the outside of the bag and tack (baste) together all round.

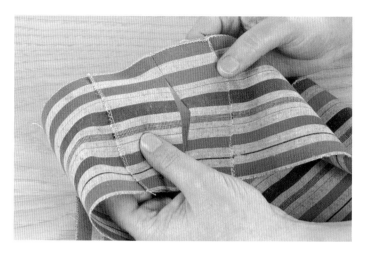

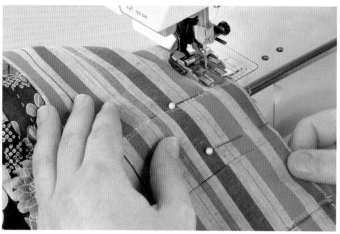

12 *Making the drawstring channel:* Zigzag the ends of the 31in x 3½in striped cotton strip. Sew the ends together to make a loop, with a 2in seam allowance, sewing only the first and last ¾in of the seam to leave a gap for the drawstring. Press the seam open and machine sew the wide seam allowance to the drawstring channel loop.

13 Pin the loop of fabric to the top of the bag, as shown, lining up the loop seam with the centre front, and machine sew it to the bag. Press the seam towards the drawstring loop, fold under a ¼in hem and fold the band to the inside of the bag. Hand sew the hem in place (see Hemming stitch, page 113).

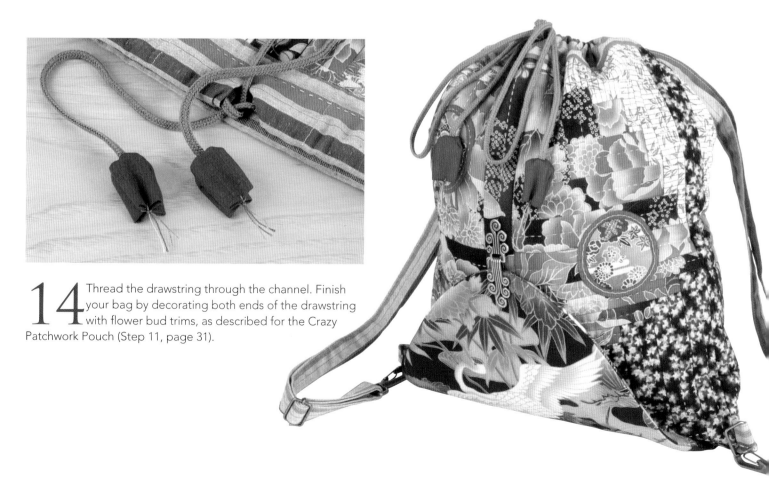

14 Thread the drawstring through the channel. Finish your bag by decorating both ends of the drawstring with flower bud trims, as described for the Crazy Patchwork Pouch (Step 11, page 31).

BATIK BOTTLE TIDY

Here's a handy way to carry up to four bottles, for parties, picnics or shopping. The bag is made as a flat panel, with four patchwork sections, folded and stitched. A fabric divider keeps bottles in place and allows for bigger bottles too. Bright batiks with butterflies and abstract patterns give the bag a summery mood. The Flying Geese patchwork is easy, machine quilted in the ditch to emphasize the piecing, while the striped binding over the seams is a bright finishing touch.

Batik fabrics are dyed with shaded colours that can vary widely over the fabric area, so you will find that just two batiks give plenty of variety for the patchwork.

You Will Need

(Seam allowances are included)

- Thirty-two 1¾in x 3½in Flying Geese units from:
  - thirty-two 2¼in x 4in rectangles
  - sixty-four 2¼in squares
- Two 21in x 4in batik pieces for straps
- Two 10in squares of contrasting batik for inner divider

- One 12in square of denim for bag base
- Four 8in squares of backing fabric
- Four 8in squares of 2oz cotton wadding (batting)
- One 27in square of batik lining fabric
- Two 21in x 4in lengths of medium iron-on interfacing, for straps

- One 7in square of pelmet interfacing, for inside bag base
- Four 19½in x 2in bias-cut strips (see page 107) for double bias binding
- Sewing and quilting threads to tone with patchwork

Making the Patchwork

1 Begin by making thirty-two Flying Geese, finished size 1¾in x 3½in (see Flying Geese page 101). Sew two strips of four Flying Geese for each side of the bag, then sew the two strips together, noting that the triangles point *up* on the left-hand side of the panel and *down* on the right, as shown in **Fig 1**.

Fig 1 Bottle Tidy panel layout

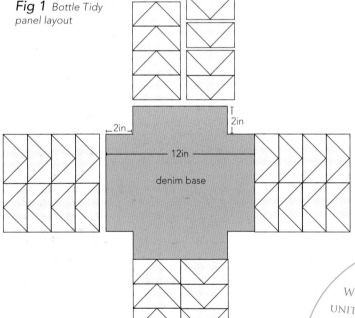

2in

2in

12in

denim base

2 Using the wadding (batting) and backing fabric, make a quilt sandwich (see page 104), and machine quilt in the ditch along all seam lines (see page 104). Repeat for each of the four sides.

Tip

When making Flying Geese units, if you sew a second line ½in from the first on the excess fabric and cut between the two lines, you can make little triangle squares as you go. I used mine to make the pinwheel blocks and sawtooth borders for the Batik Butterfly bag on page 13.

CONSTRUCTING THE BAG

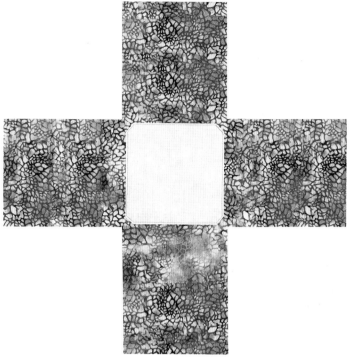

3 *Making the bag outer panel:* Cut 2in squares out of each corner of the 12in square of denim. Using the four patchwork panels, machine sew one panel to each side of the denim square right sides together, as shown above. Press seams alternately towards the denim and the patchwork. The bag panel is now complete.

4 *Making the lining:* Using the bag panel as a pattern, cut the 27in square piece of batik lining fabric to the same size, to form a cross shape. Cut a small diagonal piece, approximately ½in, from each corner of the 7in square of pelmet interfacing. Pin the interfacing to the centre of the wrong side of the lining, as shown above, and machine sew to the lining.

5 *Making the lining divider:* With right sides together, fold each 10in square of contrasting batik in half and machine sew into a tube. Turn each tube right side out, press and then overlock each end on both tubes. On the right side of the lining, mark a line down the centre of each side and another parallel to each end of the cross shape, 1½in from the end – the lines will form a T shape. With the divider seam towards the centre of the cross shape, line up the end of each divider with the line down the centre of each side and pin, as shown.

6 Machine sew the first divider to the side of the lining, with a scant ¼in seam. Flip the divider over, press and machine sew another line, ¼in from the folded edge, to neaten the join. Repeat for the second divider.

7 Sew the lining divider to the next side of the lining, repeating part of Step 5 and Step 6. Once the divider is attached to the next side, you will be unable to lay the lining flat, as the two adjacent sides will be joined to each other by the divider. Repeat for the second divider.

8 *Sewing the lining into the bag:* With right sides together, pin the bag panel to the lining fabric, along the edges of the cross only i.e., the points of the cross, and machine sew together. This will become the top of the bag. Press seams towards the lining fabric.

9 Turn the bag right side out, though any of the gaps between the bag panel and the lining. Because the top edges of the bag and the lining are already sewn together, any of the gaps can be used to turn it out through, as shown in this sequence. Press the bag panel and lining seam around the top of the bag.

IDEA

I USED STRIPED FABRIC TO MAKE A DYNAMIC DIAGONAL BIAS BINDING, BUT USE BINDING CUT ON THE STRAIGHT GRAIN IF YOU PREFER.

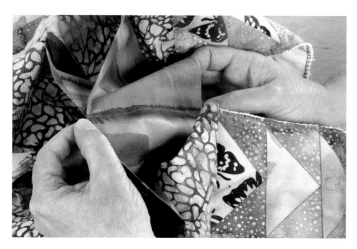

10 Finish sewing the lining divider, by stitching the two pieces together down the centre: mark the centre of each piece with a vertical line, pin the lines together and machine sew down the line, as shown (see also **Fig 2**).

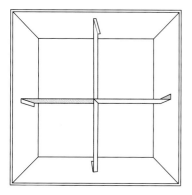

Fig 2 Bottle Tidy divider in place

11 *Sewing the bag seams:* Pin the lining to the bag along all the unsewn edges, then each side of the cross to the next side, along the edge, with the right side of the patchwork on the outside of the bag. Pin and machine sew each seam in turn, sewing a scant ¼in seam. Overlock or zigzag each seam after sewing. Make and sew the bias binding to cover each bag seam, as for the Quilter's Portfolio (Step 10, page 13).

12 *Making the handles:* Using two 21in x 4in batik pieces and the matching pieces of interfacing, make the straps, as described for the Quilter's Pocket Book (Step 4, page 24). Machine sew each strap, sewing one line very close to each long edge. Pin one strap to the first side of the bag, with the end pointing upwards, ½in from the bag top. Machine sew the strap through the bag outer and lining, stitching ¾in from the bag top. Repeat to sew the strap to the next side of the bag and repeat with the second strap. Fold each strap upwards, over its raw edge end and machine sew a cross in a figure of eight (see Attaching straps and D-rings, page 110).

GARDEN TIDY

This delightful gardener's version of the tidy has pockets in the sides, made with extra fabric patches sewn along the edges of the patchwork sides, before stitching to the base panel. Leafy fabrics and rustic wooden buttons enhance the garden theme (see Mail-Order Suppliers, page 118). The fabric divider is left out, so there is plenty of room for your trowel and twine – and maybe a bottle of lemonade for hot days!

Tringle Rucksack

Why 'tringle'? – the rounded corners mean it's not quite a triangle! I designed the tringle as a neat backpack to keep the shoulders free. Distressed denim and checked flannel contribute to a relaxed theme, with machine quilting co-ordinating with the Tuck-In Shoulder Bag on page 14. The patchwork panels are two rectangles cut to shape after quilting while the bias-bound front edge gives the bag rigidity. The Sepia Tringle variation on page 73 co-ordinates with three other bags in the book (see pages 20, 48 and 89).

Adjust the strap length on this bag with the side buckle and eyelets. Because the strap runs freely through the D-ring at the top, the bag is easy to put on and is comfortable to wear.

YOU WILL NEED

(Unless otherwise stated, add seam allowances to fabric and wadding sizes – see page 5)

- Two 14in x 8in checkerboard patchwork panels from fifty-six 2in squares
- One 40½in x 3½in denim strip for bag gusset (seam allowances included)
- Two 15in x 9in backing pieces for patchwork panels
- Two 15in x 9in pieces of 2oz cotton wadding (batting)
- Lining fabric pieces:
  – one 40½in x 3½in for gusset (seam allowances included)
  – one 15in x 17in for back and front
- One 2in x 45in bias-cut fabric strip
- 2in fabric strips (seam allowances included):
  – one 60in x 2in for strap
  – one 4½in x 2in for buckle loop
- 1in fabric strips (seam allowances included):
  – one 14½in x 1in for back panel sashing
  – two 3in x 1in for ends of zip
- 1in wide webbing:
  – one 60in length for strap

- one 4½in length for buckle loop
- one 3in length for D-ring loop
- One 1in antique brass buckle
- One 1in antique brass D-ring
- Three one-part eyelets
- Sewing and quilting threads to tone with patchwork
- Shaded machine embroidery or jeans thread
- Machine embroidery needle suitable for machine embroidery or jeans thread
- 3½in and 4½in diameter circle templates

MAKING THE PATCHWORK

1 Begin by making two 14in x 8in checkerboard patchwork panels. Each block is made from an assortment of 2in squares (finished size), with a few triangle squares mixed in (see Patchwork Techniques from page 97). Try to arrange the squares at random. Machine sew strips of four squares together, then sew strips into pairs and then into panels, as shown in **Fig 1**. Repeat for the second panel.

TIP

FOR THE SQUARES IN STEP 1, CUT 2½IN STRIPS AND THEN CUT SQUARES FROM THE STRIPS. IF YOU HAVE ALREADY MADE THE TUCK-IN SHOULDER BAG (PAGE 14), YOU WILL HAVE A COUPLE OF TRIANGLE SQUARES LEFT OVER AND PROBABLY SOME STRIPS TOO, SO USE THESE UP ON THE TRINGLE!

Fig 1 Patchwork panels for the front and back of the bag. The white dashed lines show the shapes to be cut out

2 With one patchwork panel, wadding (batting) and backing, make a quilt sandwich (see page 104) and then machine quilt (page 104). Using shaded machine embroidery or jeans thread, quilt each panel in the ditch, then quilt three parallel diagonal lines, as shown in the detail photograph above. Stitch the centre diagonal lines first, then sew a line on either side, about ¼in apart, using the width of the machine foot as your guide. Trim the panels to measure 14½in x 8½in (including seam allowance).

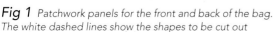

Constructing the Bag

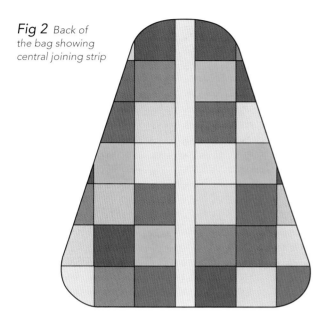

Fig 2 *Back of the bag showing central joining strip*

3 *Shaping the panels:* Cut the first patchwork panel into two right-angled triangles, following the white dashed lines in Fig 1. Use a 4½in circle template to draw the curve at the narrow end of the triangle and a 3½in circle to draw the curve at the wide end. Cut around the curves. Use the shapes you have already cut as templates to cut out the second panel, placing the panel pieces right sides together when you cut. Remember, one panel must be cut as a *mirror image* of the other. Sew all round each patchwork panel and overlock or zigzag the edges. Decide which two panels you will use for the back. Join them with the 14½in x 1in fabric strip, as shown in **Fig 2**. Pin and machine sew the strip to the centre edge of one piece, press towards the sashing and sew to the other half of the back. Use the three patchwork pieces as patterns to cut out the lining pieces from the 15in x 17in piece, arranging the back panel in the centre with the two front panels on either side (similar to Fig 1).

4 *Inserting the zip:* Fold one 3in x 1in fabric strip in half across the width and machine sew to the end of the zip tape. Repeat with the other 3in x 1in strip at the other end of the zip. Place the completed zip strip and front right panel right sides together, lining up the edge of the zip tape with the edge of the patchwork panel. Make sure the zip pull is at the top of the triangle. Pin and tack (baste) in place using diagonal tacking stitches (see Inserting zips, page 108). Don't tack over the zip teeth because you will need to partly open the zip when machine sewing.

5 Place one lining triangle right sides together with the front panel from Step 4, as shown. Pin and tack (baste) the lining over the back of the zip and machine sew the zip in place.

6 Machine sew the zip to the other half of the front panel and front lining, as before, first tacking the zip to the second front panel and then tacking the lining to that.

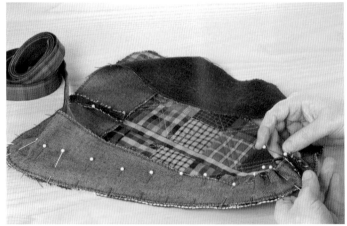

7 *Making buckle loop, D-ring loop and strap:* Using the 2in fabric strips and 1in wide webbing, follow the method shown for the Leafy Satchel loops and straps (Step 4, page 39 and Step 11, page 40), omitting the wadding (batting) strip from the strap. Thread the D-ring on to the shortest completed loop and fold the loop so the webbing is inside. Pin to the centre top of the back panel and tack (baste). Make a small hole for the buckle prong and thread the buckle on to its loop, pushing the prong through the hole. Pin and tack, lining up the edge of the loop with the bottom edge of the second patchwork square, as shown. Pin and tack the long strap to the opposite edge of the back panel.

8 *Making the gusset and gusset lining:* Cut the 40½in x 3½in denim gusset and lining pieces to shape, following the dimensions in **Fig 3** below. These may be made from two pieces seamed across the fold line, as indicated in the diagram. With right sides together, sew the ends of each piece together to make a loop. Mark the centre top and centre bottom of the gusset strip and the centre top and bottom of the back panel. Pin the gusset to the back panel at top and bottom, right side to right side. Continue pinning, easing the gusset to the side panel then tack (baste) together, as shown below. Turn the back of the bag over and repeat with the lining. Machine sew the gusset and gusset lining to the back panel at the same time. Lay the bag on its back, line up the edges of the gusset and the gusset lining and pin and tack (baste) the edges together.

> ### TIP
> WHEN MAKING THE LONG STRAP YOU MAY NEED TO JOIN FABRIC. SEW SHORTER STRIPS TOGETHER, WITH THE SEAM AT A 45-DEGREE ANGLE, AS IF PIECING BINDING STRIPS (SEE MAKING AND ATTACHING BINDINGS, PAGE 107) AND PRESS OPEN. THE EXTRA THICKNESS AT THE SEAM WILL BE MORE EVENLY DISTRIBUTED AND THE WEBBING WILL REINFORCE THE SEAM.

> ### IDEA
> USE THE DENIM LEFT OVER FROM CUTTING OUT THE BAG STRAPS AND TOP SECTIONS FOR THE GUSSET STRIP ON THE TUCK-IN SHOULDER BAG (PAGE 14).

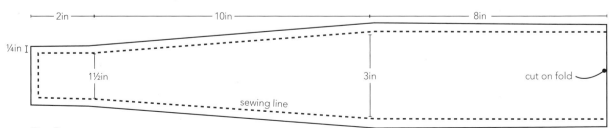

Fig 3 Shaping the gusset (not to scale) – cut one in denim

9 *Attaching the front panel:* Place the front panel right side up on the back of the bag. The last construction seam is sewn on the outside and is covered with bias binding. Centre and pin the gusset and the gusset lining to the front panel. Pin all round and tack (baste). Machine sew the seam, sewing a scant ¼in so the seam will be hidden by the bias binding.

10 Using the bias-cut strips, make double bias binding (see Making and attaching bindings, page 107). Pin and machine sew the binding around the edge of the each panel, being careful not to stretch the binding. Start and finish along a straight edge, so the ends of the bias can be joined smoothly. When the machine stitching is complete, fold the bias binding over and hem stitch it in place all around the bag panel.

Idea

FOR AN ALTERNATIVE METHOD OF ATTACHING THE FRONT PANEL AND SEWING THE FIRST STAGE OF THE BIAS BINDING IN ONE, PIN AND TACK (BASTE) THE BIAS BINDING TO THE FRONT PANEL, THEN FOLLOW STEP 9, SEWING THE BINDING, THE FRONT PANEL AND THE GUSSET/GUSSET LINING TOGETHER WITH A ¼IN SEAM. IF YOU NEED TO REPLACE THE BINDING SOMETIME IN THE FUTURE, JUST REMEMBER THE STITCHING IS ALSO HOLDING THE BAG TOGETHER!

11 Try the bag on, checking the length of the strap. Decide where you want to place the three eyelets into the long strap. Finish your bag by inserting the eyelets using a setting tool or eyelet pliers.

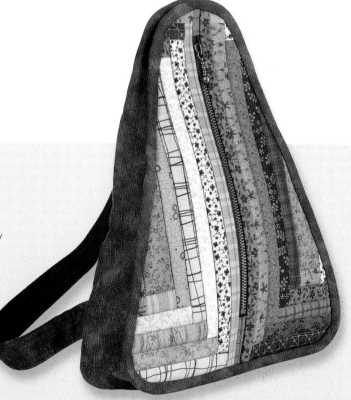

SEPIA TRINGLE

This three-quarter size version of the tringle co-ordinates with the sepia bags on pages 20, 48 and 89. An elongated Log Cabin block is the starting point for each triangle, simply quilted in the ditch. Brown marbled cotton used for bias binding was interlined with calico to give it enough body for use as a gusset. For adult use, the strap is a few inches longer than the denim and plaid tringle but, with a shorter strap, this three-quarter size bag would be suitable for a child.

BOLLYWOOD HANDBAG

Get some Bollywood glamour with twinkling shisha mirrors and fabrics woven with gold threads. This cute evening bag is reminiscent of retro travel holdalls, with outer pockets and a zip fastener, only on a smaller scale. I foundation pieced the patchwork gusset strip from silk sample squares and scraps, contrasting the brightly coloured silks with woven silk brocade and a neutral cream unbleached silk and cotton mix.

A small amount of free-motion machine quilting in a wiggling vermicelli pattern on the brocade, raw-edge appliqué zigzags and machine couched sparkly chainette mean there's plenty of detail on this gorgeous bag. Only tiny amounts of fabric are needed, so a little goes a long way – for maximum impact!

You Will Need

(Unless otherwise stated, add seam allowances to all fabric and wadding sizes – see page 5)

- Two 3½in x 6in appliqué pocket panels:
  - two 3½in x 6in striped fabric
  - two 3in x 6½in cream muslin (no seam allowance needed)
- One 11½in x 2in stitch and flip patchwork panel from silk scraps for gusset
- Two 4½in x 6in metallic brocade for side panels
- Cream silk/cotton mix:
  - one 4in x 7½in for zigzag appliqué (no seam allowance needed)
  - two 3½in x 6in for pocket lining

- two 1½in x 8½in for zip gusset (seam allowance included)
- Backing fabric (no seam allowance needed):
  - two 4in x 7in
  - two 5in x 7in
  - one 12in x 2½in
- 2oz cotton wadding (batting) (no seam allowances needed):
  - two 4in x 7in
  - two 5in x 7in
  - one 12in x 2½in
- Lining fabric (allowances included):
  - two 5in x 6½in for side panels
  - two 8½in x 2in for zip strip
  - one 11½in x 2in for gusset

- Two 1½in x 8½in lightweight iron-on interfacing
- 8in zip
- Ten plastic shisha mirrors
- 30in metallic viscose chainette cord
- Two 12in lengths of rouleau braid or similar for handles
- Sewing and quilting threads to tone with patchwork
- Shaded fine cotton perlé embroidery thread
- 2½in diameter circle template

Tip

Couching cord by machine is easy if you have a cording foot. The cord is guided through a slot or hole, keeping it in position for stitching over with zigzag or blanket stitch.

Making the Patchwork

1 Begin by making two 3½in x 6in appliquéd and embellished pocket panels. Pin one 3½in x 6in piece of striped fabric to one 3½in x 6in piece of backing fabric, wrong sides together. Pin one piece of cream muslin on top, lining up with the top edge of the pocket panel. Repeat for the second panel.

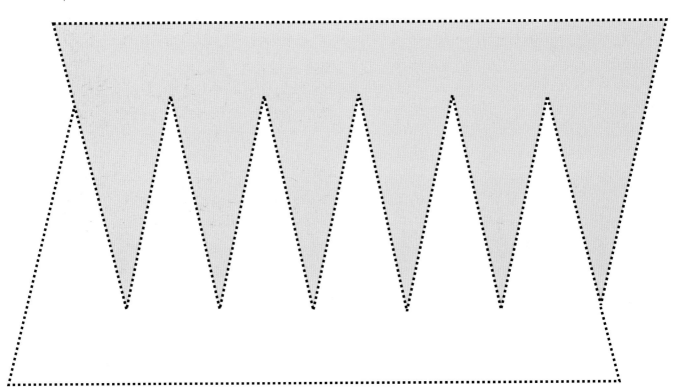

Fig 1 Template for both pieces of zigzag appliqué (shown actual size). Cut out of cream fabric following the dotted lines

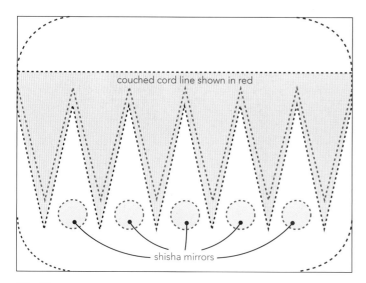

couched cord line shown in red

shisha mirrors

Fig 2 Complete side panel with pocket

2 Following **Fig 1** cut the zigzag appliqué from one 4in x 7½in piece of silk/cotton mix. Pin over the muslin, lining up with the panel top. Machine sew the appliqué in place, stitching about ⅛in from the edge. Couch metallic viscose chainette over the machine stitches using machine zigzag (**Fig 2**). Machine sew around the panel, ⅛in from edge, trim to measure 5in x 6½in (including seam allowances) and overlock or zigzag the edges. Using embroidery scissors, carefully cut away the muslin into the zigzag appliqué points. Using shaded perlé thread hand quilt with big stitch quilting (page 106), following the fabric stripes.

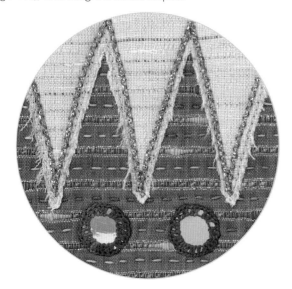

4 Make a stitch and flip strip for the gusset, using scraps of silk and the 12in x 2½in piece of backing fabric (see Stitch and flip strip, page 101). Trim the finished strip to measure 11½ x 2in and quilt with parallel lines ⅛in apart. Overlock or zigzag the edges.

TIP

PLASTIC SHISHA MIRRORS ARE MUCH EASIER TO STITCH THAN TRADITIONAL INDIAN GLASS MIRRORS AND DON'T BREAK. FOR EVEN EASIER SHISHA, BUY THE ONES WITH READY-MADE MACHINE EMBROIDERED RINGS AND SEW THE RINGS ON WITH A FEW STITCHES.

3 Sew the shisha mirrors to both panels, positioning them as shown in Fig 2 and described in **Fig 3**, below.

Fig 3 Attaching shisha mirrors

Figs 3a–e Hold the shisha mirror in place temporarily with double-sided tape or a spot of PVA glue. Begin with a knot on the back of work and, starting at 1, follow the numbered stitching sequence in Figs 3a to 3e to make a mesh over the shisha mirror

Fig 3f Turn the panel so point 9 is at the lower left. Slip the needle from above behind the thread intersection and pull through

Fig 3g Working clockwise, take a small stitch in the panel fabric, loop the working thread under the needle and pull the needle through

Fig 3h Slip the needle behind the thread mesh and pull through

Fig 3i Insert the needle into the lower left loop, take a small stitch through the fabric and pull through. Repeat the stitch, working clockwise around the mirror

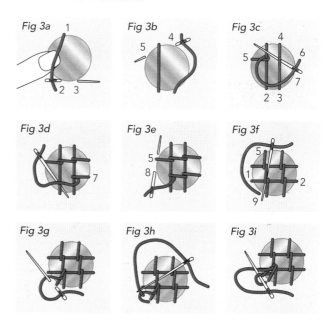

5 Using one 4½in x 6in piece of metallic brocade, wadding (batting) and backing, make a quilt sandwich (see page 104) and then free-motion machine quilt (page 104) in a vermicelli pattern of random wiggly lines all over the side panel. Trim the finished side panel to measure 5in x 6½in (including seam allowances). Using a 2½in circle template, mark and trim the corners into neat curves. Machine sew and overlock edges.

BOLLYWOOD HANDBAG   77

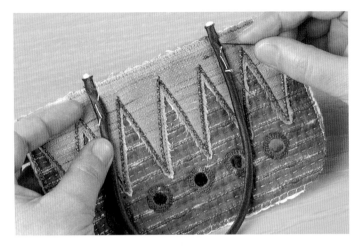

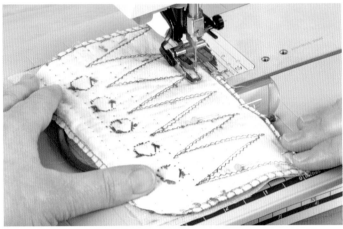

6 *Attaching the handles:* Pin and tack (baste) one 12in length of rouleau braid to the top of the pocket panel, as shown. Line up the handle with the centre top of the second triangle zigzag. The handle will be caught in the seam when the pocket lining is sewn in.

7 Place a pocket panel and a pocket lining piece right sides together, pin and machine sew. Sew across the handles again, ⅛in from fabric edge. Fold the lining behind the pocket front, line up the edges, pin and machine sew along the raw edges. Repeat Steps 5–7 with the second pocket panel.

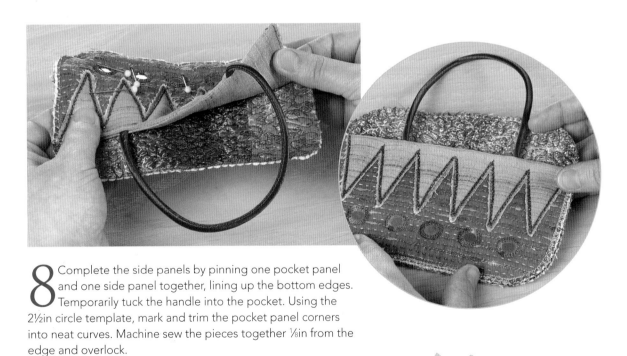

8 Complete the side panels by pinning one pocket panel and one side panel together, lining up the bottom edges. Temporarily tuck the handle into the pocket. Using the 2½in circle template, mark and trim the pocket panel corners into neat curves. Machine sew the pieces together ⅛in from the edge and overlock.

Idea

You could sew press studs or use magnetic purse fasteners to close the side pockets. Alternatively, a button loop could be added at the same time as the handles (see Leafy Satchel, Step 6, page 39).

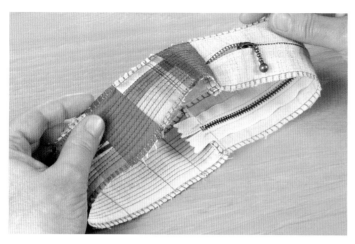

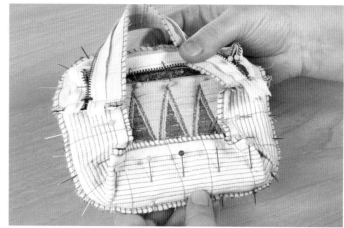

9 *Making the bag gusset:* Iron the interfacing to the back of the two 1½in x 8½in pieces for the zip gusset. Using the two panels and an 8in zip, insert the zip. Tack (baste) the two pieces right sides together ½in from the edge and press open. On the wrong side, tack the zip in place and machine sew (see Inserting a zip invisibly, page 109). With right sides together, machine sew the zip section to the patchwork gusset strip made in Step 4. Press towards the patchwork strip.

10 *Assembling the bag:* Mark the centre top and centre bottom of the gusset strip and the first side panel. Pin the gusset to the side panel at the top and at the bottom, making sure the side panel is the right way up! Continue pinning, easing the gusset to the side panel. Now machine sew together, then press towards the patchwork panel. Repeat with the other side panel.

11 *Making and inserting the lining:* Press a ½in hem along the long side of each 11½in x 2in lining piece – these pieces will line the zip part of the gusset. Assemble the lining the same way as the outside of the bag, machine sewing the 11½in long pieces to the 8½in x 2in piece to make the lining gusset strip. Use the 2½in circle template to mark and trim the lining side panel corners into neat curves. Sew the lining gusset to the side panels. With the bag inside out and lining right side out, place the bag inside the lining. Smooth the lining over the bag, making sure the corners and seams line up. Pin, tack (baste) and slipstitch the lining to the back of the zip, taking care not to sew too close to the teeth. Turn the bag right side out to finish.

RETRO TRAVELLER

A collection of retro fabric prints provided a starting point for a much bigger version of the Bollywood Handbag. The bag's dimensions were multiplied by three, to make a bag measuring 13½in x 18in x 4½in – useful for long weekends or airline hand luggage. I used synthetic faux suede fabric for the gusset to contrast with the patchwork prints. Patterns inspired by 1950s designs were free-motion quilted on the pocket panels, with hand quilted background rectangles, and a machine quilted grid on the blue floral print. For a more rigid bag, the gusset and side panels are sewn together with the seams on the outside, like the front of the Tringle Rucksack on page 68.

Starry Backpack

Is there a star in your life who would appreciate this backpack? Or maybe you feel in need of a little star treatment yourself? A galaxy of stars and metallic prints set the theme, with traditional star blocks on the pockets, star buttons and a shiny leather appliqué star on the top. The bottom of the sack is also made of leather, although denim or canvas would be equally strong. Pockets with button loops provide accessible storage for smaller items, with deep, pleated side pockets too.

This roomy backpack would be great for dance or sports wear or perhaps for clothes and accessories if you're planning a night away from home. Machine quilting in metallic threads adds to the sparkle of this fun yet functional creation.

YOU WILL NEED

(Unless otherwise stated, add seam allowances to all fabric and wadding sizes – see page 5)

- Two 13in x 12in patchwork panels from twelve 13in x 1in strips, for back and front
- Two 13in x 4in patchwork panels from four 13in x 1in strips, for sides
- One 7in x 12in patchwork panel for front pocket:
  – two 6in square Four-Patch Weave blocks
  – one 1in x 12in strip
- Two 9in x 4in patchwork panels for side pockets:
  – four 4in square Eight-Point Stars
  – two 1in x 6in strips
  – four 1in x 8in strips
- Metallic leather (seam allowance included):
  – one 18½in x 8½in for base
  – one 5in square for appliqué star
- Fabric pieces (seam allowance included):
  – one 32½in x 3½in for eyelet band

  – two 18in x 3in for straps
  – one 7in x 8in for top flap
- Backing fabric:
  – one 8in x 13in for front pocket
  – one 7in x 8in for top flap
  – two 10in x 5in for side pockets
  – two 14in x 13in for back and front
  – two 14in x 5in for sides
- 'Request' weight cotton wadding (batting):
  – one 8in x 13in for front pocket
  – one 7in x 8in for top flap
  – two 10in x 5in for side pockets
  – two 14in x 13in for back and front
  – two 14in x 5in for sides
- Main lining fabric:
  – two 13in x 12in for front and back
  – two 13in x 4in for sides
  – one 18½in x 8½in for base (seam allowance included)
- Pocket and flap lining fabric:
  – one 7in x 12in for front pocket
  – two 9in x 4in for side pockets
  – one 7in x 8in for top flap
- Four 3½in x 1in strips for button loops

(seam allowance included)
- Lightweight iron-on interfacing (seam allowances not required):
  – one 32in x 3in for eyelet band
  – two 18in x 3in for straps
- One 2in x 30in bias-cut fabric strip for flap binding
- Four star-shaped buttons 1in wide
- 1in wide webbing:
  – two 13in lengths for lower strap
  – two 30in lengths for upper strap
- Two 1in antique nickel slide adjusters
- Twelve two-part silver eyelets, with setting tool
- One 40in length of cord, for drawstring
- Two silver metal bobble ends for drawstring
- One silver metal two-part decorative hook fastener
- Sewing and quilting threads to tone with patchwork
- Metallic machine embroidery thread
- Machine embroidery needle suitable for metallic thread

MAKING THE PATCHWORK

1 Begin by making two 13in x 12in and two 13in x 4in patchwork panels from twelve 1in strips (finished size), for back, front and sides. With the wadding (batting) and backing, make a quilt sandwich (page 104) and then machine quilt (page 104). Quilt each panel in the ditch, then at ¼in intervals along each strip. Use metallic thread and a fancy machine stitch to quilt random diagonal lines and zigzags.

TIP

ON SOME SEAMS YOU WILL NEED TO MACHINE SEW THROUGH UP TO FOUR QUILTED LAYERS, SO USE ONLY THIN 'REQUEST' WEIGHT WADDING (BATTING). CHECK YOUR MACHINE CAN STITCH THROUGH SO MANY LAYERS FIRST! TRY USING A DENIM NEEDLE, QUILTING NEEDLE OR HEAVIER UNIVERSAL MACHINE NEEDLE. ALTERNATIVELY, OMIT WADDING FROM THE BAG POCKETS.

2 Make two 6in Four-Patch Weave and four 4in Eight-Point Star blocks. Each block is made from an assortment of 1in strips, squares and Flying Geese units (finished sizes) – see Patchwork Techniques beginning on page 97 and the Block Library page 116.

3 To complete the patchwork panel for the front pocket, machine sew the two 6in blocks together into one patchwork panel (**Fig 1**) and then sew a 1in x 12in strip along the front top pocket.

Four-Patch Weave block

Eight-Point Star block

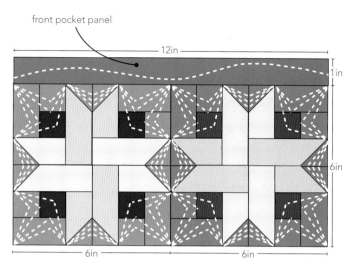

Fig 1 *Quilting pattern (shown in white dashed lines) for front pocket*

4 Machine sew two 4in blocks together into one patchwork panel, and then sew one 1in x 8in strip to either side and a 1in x 6in strip along the top for each side pocket (**Fig 2**).

5 Make a quilt sandwich and then machine quilt (see page 104). Quilt in the ditch around the blocks and the central stars. Use a metallic thread to quilt around the stars, following the white dashed lines in Figs 1 and 2. Use a fancy machine stitch to quilt the wavy lines across the top of each panel.

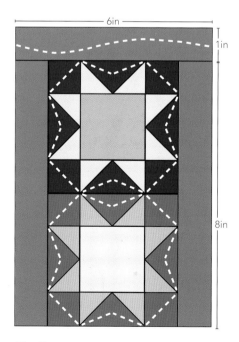

Fig 2 *Quilting pattern (shown in white dashed lines) for side pockets*

TIP

WHEN WORKING WITH METALLIC THREADS, STITCH MORE SLOWLY THAN USUAL AND LOOSEN THE TOP TENSION ON YOUR MACHINE SLIGHTLY TO AVOID SNAPPING OR SHREDDING THE THREAD.

6 *Assembling the pockets:* Using the four 3½in x 1in strips and following the folding diagrams for the Quilter's Pocket Book (page 24), make the button loops. Machine sew along each loop twice, close to the edge. Fold each loop in half and tack (baste) one loop to the centre top of each side pocket, as shown. The front pocket has two loops, centred above each star block. Remember to check that the button can go through the loops easily. Pin the pocket lining right sides together along the top of each pocket panel and machine sew together. Remove tacking and press. Fold over the lining against the back of the pocket, machine sew across the pocket top and around all the sides ⅛in from the edge. Overlock or zigzag the bottom edge of the front pocket.

7 Pin one side pocket to one side panel along the long edges only, lining up the bottom of the pocket with the bottom of the panel and tacking (basting) along the long edges. Repeat with the second side panel and pocket.

Idea

ADD TO THE SPARKLY EFFECT OF THE METALLIC THREADS BY EMBELLISHING THE PATCHWORK STARS WITH TINY BEADS OR SEQUINS.

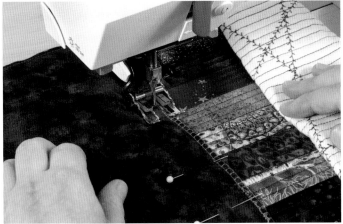

8 Make a small pleat on either side of the side pocket, as shown, making sure the fold at the side of the pocket is ⅜in from the side edge, so it can't be caught in the side seam. Pin and tack (baste) in place. Repeat this pleating for the second side pocket.

9 Mark a line across the front panel, 3in up from the bottom edge, with right sides together, line up the bottom of the front pocket on this line with the pocket pointing downwards (it will overlap the front panel's bottom edge). Pin and machine sew together. Fold up the pocket, lining up with the sides of the front panel and tack (baste). Pin and machine sew up the centre of the pocket, thus creating two pockets.

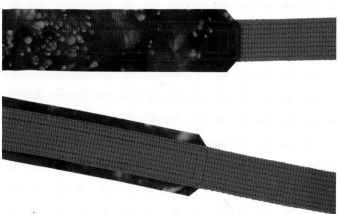

10

Making the straps: Thread one adjustable slide on to each of the 13in long webbing pieces, fold each in half, pin and tack the raw ends to the back panel, 1in up from the bottom edge.

Fig 3 Making the straps

Fig 3a

crease fold line

Fig 3b

fold long
edge to centre

Fig 3c

Fig 3d

fold corners in

Fig 3e

fold corners in

Fig 3f

stitch webbing in place

11

Iron one 18in x 3in interfacing piece to each 18in x 3in upper strap. Fold the first strap in half along its length, press and use the crease line to fold the long edges to the centre. At one end, fold the corners in, press and then fold in the end, as shown in **Fig 3**. Tack (baste) and fold in place. Pin one 30in long piece of webbing along the strap, covering raw edges along the centre, and stitch together with two parallel rows. Position the straps at the top of the back panel, 1½in either side of the panel centre, with the unfinished ends overlapping the panel edge by ¼in. Pin and tack the straps.

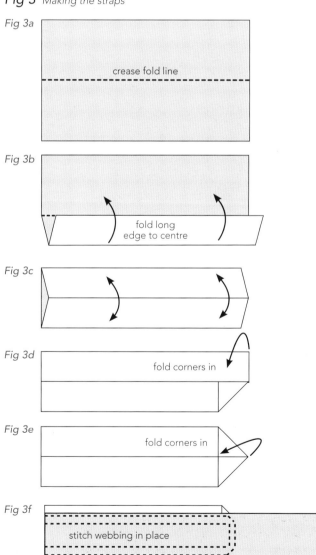

12

Assembling the bag: Cut 2in squares from each corner of the 18½in x 8½in silver leather base panel. Following the layout in **Fig 4** overleaf, prepare to stitch the front, back and side panels to the leather base. Pins would leave holes in the leather, so hold the pieces in place with paperclips. Clip leather and patchwork panels right sides together and stitch. Press the seams – side panels towards the base, front and back seams towards the patchwork. Use a pressing cloth and try not to press the metallic leather.

IDEA

IF YOU PREFER NOT TO USE LEATHER, SELECT A TOUGH
FABRIC FOR THE BASE, SUCH AS DENIM, CORDUROY
OR CANVAS, OR TRY SYNTHETIC 'DRESS' LEATHER.

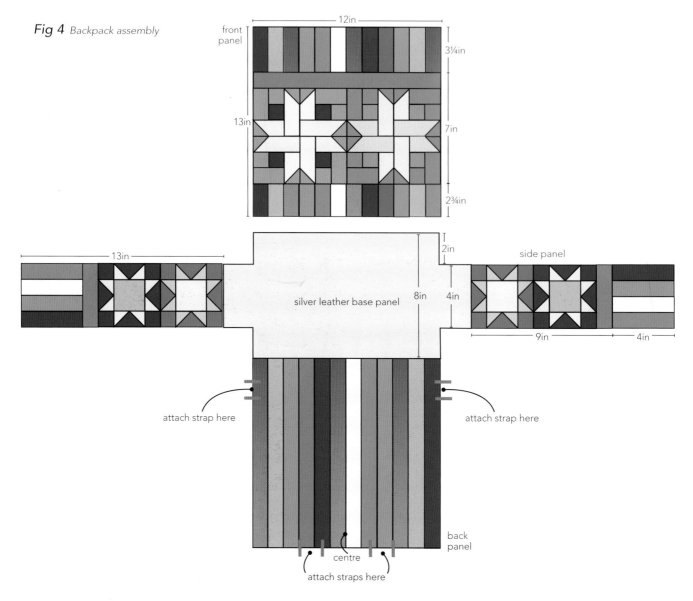

Fig 4 *Backpack assembly*

front panel

12in

3¼in

13in

7in

2¾in

13in

2in

silver leather base panel

8in

4in

side panel

9in

4in

attach strap here

attach strap here

attach strap here

centre

attach straps here

back panel

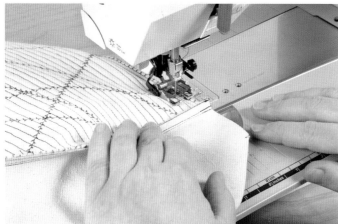

13 Sew the bag side seams. Fold the bag, pin one side panel to the front panel and machine stitch. (See Tip on page 82 about sewing through multiple layers.) Sew from the top of the bag towards the base. Repeat for the other three bag seams.

14 Attach the star buttons now. Mark a point behind each button loop, pin the button in place temporarily and check it will fasten. Keep the loop fairly loose on the button, so fastening the pocket won't strain the button stitches. Hand sew each button in place. Sew the loop section of the metal hook fastener to the top of the front pocket.

15 *Inserting the lining:* Cut 2in squares from the lining base fabric, as for the leather base in Step 12. Assemble the lining the same way as making the bag in Steps 12 and 13. With the bag right side out and the lining inside out, place the lining inside the bag and pin. Sew the ends of the 32½in x 3½in eyelet band right sides together to make a loop and pin to the top of the bag, as shown, lining up the band seam with the centre back. Machine sew the lining and eyelet band to the top of the bag. Press the seam towards the eyelet band, fold under a ¼in hem and fold the band to the inside of the bag. Hand sew the hem in place.

16 *Inserting the eyelets:* Following the manufacturer's instructions and using an eyelet setting tool, insert the eyelets around the top of the bag. Insert four eyelets in the back of the bag, at 3in intervals, with the first two eyelets ½in from the eyelet band seam (i.e. the centre back); two eyelets above each side panel, above the first and fourth patchwork strip, and four eyelets above the front panel. Thread cord through the eyelets, thread metal bobbles on to the ends and knot the cord ends after completing Step 17.

TIP

WHEN YOU SEW ON THE STAR YOU MAY FIND THE LEATHER SLIPS. IF THIS HAPPENS, TEMPORARILY STICK THE STAR TO THE BAG FLAP WITH A DAB OF FABRIC GLUE OR SMALL PIECES OF DOUBLE-SIDED TAPE WHILE YOU STITCH IT IN PLACE.

17 *Making and attaching the flap:* With the 7in x 8in fabric piece, wadding (batting) and backing, make a quilt sandwich (see page 104). Using the 5in square piece of silver leather, cut out a star, using the actual size pattern from **Fig 5** overleaf, and appliqué it to the flap. Hold the star in place in the centre and machine stitch around it ⅛in from the edge (see Tip, right). With metallic thread, echo quilt around the star at ¼in intervals. Using the pattern from Fig 5, trim the quilted flap to size.

18 Using the 2in x 30in bias cut strip, make double bias binding (see Making and attaching bindings page 107). Pin and machine sew the binding around the edge of the flap, being careful not to stretch the binding. Start and finish along the straight top edge, so the ends of the binding can be joined smoothly. When the machine stitching is complete, fold the bias binding over and slipstitch it in place all around the flap. Stitch the hook section of the metal fastener to the centre front edge. Pin the flap to the back of the bag, centring it on the patchwork panel, with the bias edge overlapping the join between the bag and the eyelet strip. Machine sew in place, stitching in the ditch right next to the bias binding.

Fig 5 *Patterns for the top flap (shown actual size)*

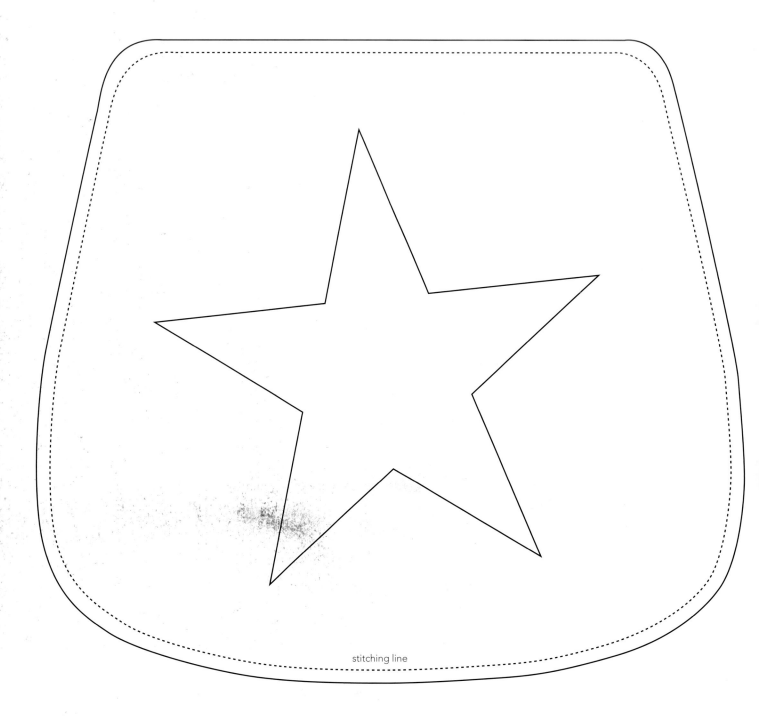

stitching line

MAGICAL MEMORIES SACK

This sack created from sepia fabrics co-ordinates with the Quilter's Pocket Book, Log Cabin Saddlebag and Sepia Tringle (pages 20, 48 and 73). Starting from the Starry Backpack, I left out the side pockets and used beige denim for the base, continuing the denim on the back panel which was cut in one with the base. The middle of each Log Cabin block is a sepia photograph, computer printed directly on the fabric (see page 50). Buttons like old-fashioned pennies were the perfect finishing touch!

EQUIPMENT AND MATERIALS

EQUIPMENT

There are many gadgets and gizmos available for today's quilter but you don't need all of them for the projects in this book! If you are a quilter already you will probably have everything you need. If not, make sure you have the following basic items.

1 Rotary Cutter
Rotary cutting has revolutionized the way patchwork is cut out, allowing quicker cutting, precision piecing without cutting templates and machine sewing with the quarter inch foot (using the cut fabric edge as a guide). Cutters come in various sizes – 28mm and 45mm blades are the most popular. Make sure the blade is clean and sharp as dull, nicked blades will skip threads and make cutting difficult. All cutters have a blade set at the end of a handle with a safety guard, operated by a clicking or squeezing action depending on the cutter. The safety guard is very important as the blade is extremely sharp, so always replace the guard after every cut. Information on rotary cutting is on page 98.

2 Cutting Mat
A self-healing cutting mat is essential for use with your rotary cutter, to protect your table and make sure your cutter blade stays sharp. There are various brands available. Choose a mat marked with imperial measurements. You can use the measurements on the mat to help you cut larger pieces but first check your mat and ruler measurements are the exactly the same. Cutting mats are tough but they can be damaged. Store flat, away from heat and direct sunlight and prolong its life by cutting smaller pieces on different areas of the mat's surface. Only use your mat with your rotary cutter – use a different mat for paper crafts.

3 Quilter's Ruler
This transparent, wider-than-average ruler marked with a grid is an indispensable tool, both for rotary cutting and for marking quilting patterns in straight lines. Imperial quilt rulers are divided into inches and fractions of an inch, to ⅛in or even 1/16in. Many have 45 and 60 degree lines too. Rulers 4½in and 6½in wide are the most useful for projects in this book. Select a ruler with clear markings and stick to the same rule throughout a project. There can be slight variations between one ruler and another, even of the same brand, and this may result in your patchwork pieces not fitting together accurately. Make sure your ruler can't slip while you are cutting. Some rulers have a raised grid or gripper dots on the wrong side to hold your fabric steady, or you could add your own self-adhesive grips.

4 Tape Measure
A good quality tape measure will be needed for measuring straps and around curves.

5 Scissors

Keep different pairs of scissors for particular jobs. You will need a large pair of sewing scissors for cutting out curves, cutting braid and other similar tasks. Reserve your best quality sewing scissors for fabric. A 'second-best' pair should be used for cutting wadding (batting), as some can blunt scissors. A small pair of embroidery scissors or thread snips makes trimming threads easy. Use paper scissors for cutting out templates for appliqué and quilting patterns.

6 Seam Ripper

This gadget is also known as a quick unpick and is often supplied in your sewing machine tool kit. It is excellent for removing tacking (basting) after inserting zips. If you make a mistake and need to use it to unpick a bag assembly seam, take care and remove one stitch at a time.

7 Fabric Markers

Fabric markers should be easy to use, easy to see and easy to remove after you have finished sewing. You will use them to mark some sewing lines in bag assembly and to mark quilting patterns, so you will need a variety of colours to contrast with your fabrics. Tailor's chalk, quilter's marking pencils and chaco liners (chalk wheels) are available in several colours. Marking pens give a good, fine line but may need to be washed out. A thin sliver of soap also marks well on dark cloth.

8 Sewing Needles and Threader

Hand and machine needles are available for many purposes and in many sizes. Use sharps for general hand sewing and betweens for hand quilting. If you find smaller betweens difficult to hold, use a sharp for hand quilting too. Crewel needles are used for embroidery and will make big stitch quilting and embellishment with embroidery threads easier. Use an appropriate machine needle for your work and change it frequently – immediately if damaged or bent, or if your machine starts skipping stitches or after several hours of stitching. I use a regular point needle size 80/11 for patchwork and bag assembly. Match your needle to your thread type (see panel page 106) – metallic, embroidery and jeans needles all have larger eyes to sew threads that would snap in a regular needle. Needles for leather have sharpened points.

9 Pins

Quilting pins are long and fine, usually with a coloured glass head. Use them when assembling bags and pin at right angles to the seam you are sewing. They can also be used for pin basting the quilt sandwich.

10 Templates

Ready-made templates in simple shapes can be used to mark quilting patterns, such as leaves, hearts and circles, or you can cut your own from cardboard or clear template plastic. Circles in various sizes are used to round off bag corners.

Iron

You will need an iron and an ironing surface for pressing patchwork and bag assembly. Press patchwork carefully to avoid distortion (see page 99). A travel iron is handy for pressing patchwork blocks. Use a steam iron to press bag assembly seams after each stage of construction.

Sewing Machine

You will need a reliable lockstitch sewing machine that can sew straight stitches and zigzag. Utility stitches and a small range of embroidery stitches are also useful. There are a number of domestic machines made for quilters that are supplied with specialized presser feet (see picture below) and a range of stitches useful for quilting, but most modern machines will be adequate. Use the correct foot for the stitch and test tension on a scrap of fabric before you begin. A walking foot (not illustrated) is necessary for smooth straight-line machine quilting on larger pieces. It helps to eliminate puckers by feeding all the layers in the quilt sandwich through at the same rate. A braiding foot is good for applying narrow cord (see the Bollywood Handbag). Use a darning or quilting foot for free-motion machine quilting – you will need to drop or cover the feed dogs. To avoid wobbly free-motion quilting lines, change the throat plate to a straight stitch plate – the zigzag throat plate has a slot for the needle to move up and down to the bobbin but a straight stitch plate only has a hole, so you can't drag the needle sideways by accident. Many machines have a 'free arm' feature, where the flat machine bed can be removed. This is really designed for dressmaking procedures but can make sewing curved sections of bags easier. If you are not familiar with your machine, work through the instruction manual or consult the machine dealer, who will also be able to supply extra machine feet.

Presser feet (left to right):
Standard straight stitch/zigzag foot – for general sewing, utility and embroidery stitches. Use for machine quilting as the wide foot covers the feed dogs adequately
Zipper foot – a narrower foot for sewing in zips and piping
Quilting guide bar – for quilting parallel lines and grids. The guide bar slots into the back of the machine foot
Quarter-inch foot – essential for accurate patchwork. Can be bought separately and may vary slightly between different manufacturers

MATERIALS

If you already enjoy quilting or dressmaking, you probably have a lot of fabric pieces and offcuts in your scrap box that would be ideal for making bags, possibly including spare patchwork blocks left over from another project. Slightly heavier curtain materials and lightweight furnishing fabrics can also be used for some parts of bags.

FABRICS

Cotton This fabric is the easiest to use for patchwork, with or without prints. Many fabrics are produced especially for patchwork and are often sold ready-cut in 'fat quarters' (a yard of fabric quartered) or 'fat eighths'. These are easy to cut and sew, don't fray too readily and can be pressed to a sharp crease. Use new fabrics for a long-lived bag. Polycotton blends and pure synthetics are not suitable for traditional patchwork as they tend to stretch and don't crease well when pressed.

Silk Handle silk with care as it frays easily and is sometimes slippery, depending on the weave. Choosing the right technique can help, such as the crazy Log Cabin on a muslin foundation used for the Crazy Patchwork Pouch. Silk is so beautiful, it's worth a little trouble!

Other fabrics Heavier fabrics can be used for the non-patchwork sections of the bags – tough denim, canvas, needlecord, faux suede and lightweight furnishing can all be used. Think about the use of the bag. If you want to be able to wash your bag, use washable fabrics. Check that fabrics can be ironed to a sharp crease, as assembling your bag can be difficult with crease-resistant fabric. Dressmaking and home furnishing shops can be a good source of interesting fabrics – often the bargain basket has a useful assortment of smaller pieces.

Backing fabrics In the quilt sandwich these are behind the wadding. The backing shows on the reverse of a patchwork quilt but is hidden in bags by the linings. A crisp backing fabric, like firm calico, would make a bag more rigid and would be harder to hand quilt. Use it for bags such as the Quilter's Portfolio or the Batik Bottle Tidy. Lightweight cottons and muslin give a softer effect and are easy to hand quilt even in big stitch, as seen in the Secret Pocket Sack.

Lining fabrics Linings protect the back of the patchwork and quilting from the bag's contents. They are best made from plainer fabrics and less 'busy' prints, as heavy patterns can camouflage the contents, especially in handbags. Solid colours can look good, co-ordinating with the main bag fabrics. Waterproof linings, like ripstop nylon, are useful for sports or beach bags.

THREADS

Sewing threads You will need good quality cotton thread for sewing patchwork and for bag assembly, with softer tacking (basting) threads for temporary stitching. Brown, sage green, dark blue, grey, beige and other neutral tones are the most useful for patchwork, co-ordinating with most colour mixtures. I do not recommend polyester as a general sewing thread because it is stronger than the cotton fibres and can eventually cut through fabric. Machine quilting shows up least with invisible nylon thread or can be emphasized with rayon or metallic threads (see the Starry Backpack). Try multicoloured cotton threads too. Jeans thread is effective for hand quilting and for topstitching, especially with denim (see the Tuck-In Shoulder Bag).

Embroidery threads Thicker threads including No.8 cotton perlé, Japanese sashiko thread and cotton à broder are excellent for hand-quilted big stitch and embroidered embellishment. You can also use multicoloured threads to accent your work (see the Secret Pocket Sack). Wind skeined threads on to cards or empty thread spools before use.

TIP

THERE ARE LOTS OF LOVELY HAND-DYED AND SHADED THREADS AVAILABLE FROM STORES, MAIL-ORDER AND CRAFT SHOWS. THESE CAN ADD A WONDERFUL, UNIQUE TOUCH TO YOUR PATCHWORK AND QUILTING – SO DO EXPERIMENT.

WADDING

Keep offcuts of wadding (batting) from larger quilted projects, as there is often enough for a bag. I store small leftovers in the original packaging for easy identification. Otherwise, quilt wadding is sold in standard sizes and by the yard. A variety of waddings are available in polyester, cotton, wool and blends, unbleached, white or black, and for hand or machine quilting. Wadding is rated by weight. Unlike choosing wadding for bed quilts, warmth is not an issue when bag making. Most of the bags were wadded with 2oz or equivalent, although thicker wadding can be used to protect a bag's contents. Match the wadding to the quilting technique – read the label or ask your supplier.

Polyester wadding This is generally easier to hand quilt through than cotton wadding but some, such as compressed 6oz polyester waddings are denser and will need to be machine quilted. Some polyester waddings are slippery for machine quilting. Polyester wadding can be high or low loft, giving a puffy or flat appearance to your quilting.

Cotton wadding This is excellent for machine quilting because it doesn't slip around in the quilt 'sandwich' of patchwork, wadding and backing. Many cotton waddings shrink when washed (by up to 5 per cent), so pre-soak the wadding and tumble dry on a low heat setting if you don't want a puckered surface and that antique look. Cotton wadding gives a flatter, low loft appearance. It can be hand quilted too.

Wool wadding This is a traditional hand quilting wadding and also the most expensive. If you love hand quilting wool wadding, use it for a soft bag. It is likely to shrink when washed.

Blended wadding Blended 80/20 waddings are now available, with 80 per cent cotton and 20 per cent polyester. There are also machine waddings with a layer of cotton scrim or muslin which prevents stretch.

FASTENERS AND NOTIONS

You will need various fasteners and notions, including zips, buttons, webbing, D-rings, cords and poppers – see the individual bag instructions for the exact requirements. As patchwork bags have become more popular, many quilt shops now stock a range of notions.

Buttons These make attractive fasteners and are available in various materials. Choose large buttons, buttons with shanks and toggles which fasten and unfasten easily. Use novelty-shaped buttons to echo the fabric theme (see the Starry Backpack).

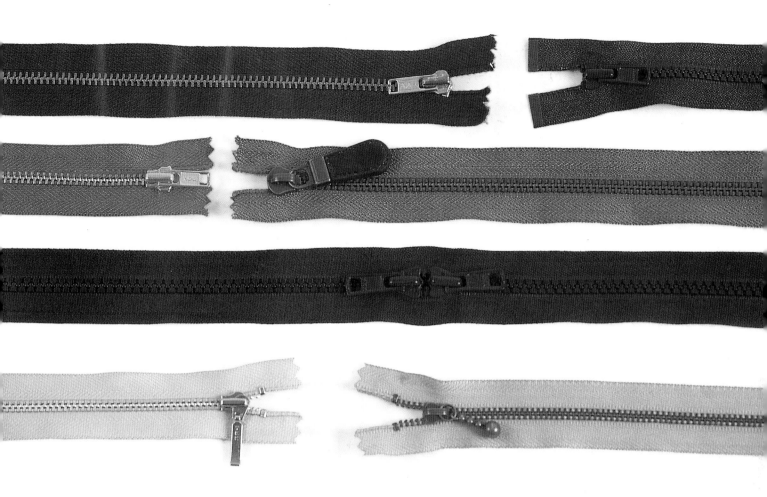

Zips These are mostly the closed-end type but open-end zips sold for jackets can be used by stitching in the ends. Choose strong, good quality zips as bag zips are opened and closed more often than zips on clothing and need to be tough. Some zips have fancy pulls or you can add tassels or beads.

Webbing This makes good straps and handles and is available in a range of colours and widths in tough nylon. Plastic buckles, used on rucksacks (sometimes called parachute clips), are made to fit standard webbing widths. Thinner cotton webbing can be sewn on to fabric to make a stronger strap (see the Leafy Satchel) or you could experiment with fancy braids. Ready-made straps and handles are increasingly available from quilt shops and give a professional look (see the Quilter's Portfolio). Try recycling a strong belt, keeping the buckle to adjust the length.

Cords and piping Use strong cord for drawstrings, threaded through a channel or eyelets (see the Pudding Bag). The cord should not be too stretchy. All but the smallest eyelets are made with two parts and are supplied in packs with eyelet tools and instructions. If you don't want to insert eyelets yourself, shoe and bag repair shops will do it for you. You can make a co-ordinated cord yourself by twisting, plaiting or braiding threads.

D-rings and clips These are available in different sizes. Check that they fit your strap or webbing at the time of purchase. If using slide adjusters, check these are the same width (see the Secret Pocket Sack). The clips are known by various names, including hipster clips and swivels.

Popper fasteners These are easy to fasten; they are made in four parts and, like eyelets, are inserted with the special tool supplied. They are sometimes sold as anorak poppers. Hook-and-loop tape (sold under the trade name 'Velcro' in the UK) is also easy to use. Large press-studs are another unobtrusive fastener.

EMBELLISHMENTS

Embellishments can make your bag really unique. Use beads, buttons, sequins and other embellishments, often best applied after the patchwork and quilting is complete but before the flat bag panels are assembled. Choose embellishments that accent and harmonize with your fabrics and the intended use of your bag (see the Bollywood Handbag).

CO-ORDINATING THE LOOK

Notions are available in various colours and materials, so remember to co-ordinate finishes for a professional look. If you can't find the fabric or notions you want in your local quilting shop, extend your searches – here are some possibilities:

Outdoor sports shops
for rucksack and tent spares, ideal for zips and clips, webbing, very strong cords and lines (sold for rock climbing).

Furnishing fabric shops
for strong fabrics for non-pieced sections of bags, long zips and zips by the yard (sold for loose covers).

Upholsterers
for long zips and zips by the yard.

Dressmaking haberdashers
for buttons, loop-and-ball fasteners, beads and trimmings.

Shoe and bag repair shops
for hipster and swivel clips, eyelet and popper insertion services.

Hardware shops
for strong webbing and cord.

And don't forget the Internet and mail order!

TECHNIQUES

You may already have patchwork and quilting experience, but for beginners this section describes all the basic patchwork, quilting and bag making techniques used in this book. I have avoided unnecessary repetition as much as possible, so some techniques that are used only once are included in the relevant bag project. Hand stitches used when making the bags are illustrated in the Stitch Library on page 112.

PATCHWORK TECHNIQUES

Many of the bags in this book have traditional patchwork blocks, so you can use up spare blocks leftover from other projects. If you are a beginner, there are lots of different patchwork techniques to whet your appetite.

Many of my favourite blocks are quick and easy to rotary cut and assemble by machine, which is perfect for bags. A standard ¼in seam allowance all round is added to all patchwork pieces when cutting out and you can sew this allowance accurately with the quarter-inch foot on your sewing machine for accurate patchwork without templates. For more ideas on blocks to use, see the Block Library on page 116.

The patchwork techniques covered in this section describe all you need to know to make the patchwork for the bags in this book and include cutting fabric strips, machine piecing techniques, speed piecing triangle squares and flying geese units, foundation piecing methods, hand piecing and appliqué.

Eight-Point Star block

Four-Patch Weave block

Preparing Fabrics

Prepare your fabrics by washing them before use in mild detergent, in case any colours run and to allow for shrinkage. Exceptions to this rule are fabrics that are dry-clean only, such as some silks (in which case remember you will not be able to wash your bag). If the fabrics lack body after washing, iron while damp with a little spray starch, but don't overdo it – too much starch leaves white marks on dark fabrics.

Cutting Fabric Strips

With reference to the three pictures, right, start with the ruler firmly on top of your fabric, squaring off uneven ends of the fabric and cutting off the tightly woven selvage. Cut with the grain of the fabric (with printed stripes and checks, cut with the pattern). Turn your cutting mat through 180 degrees and line up the relevant mark on the ruler – for example, 2½in if 2in is the finished size. Line up your rotary cutter against the ruler's edge and cut. You can cut strips very economically to standard sizes for squares and rectangles, such as 2½in squares and 1½in x 2½in rectangles from the same 2½in strip.

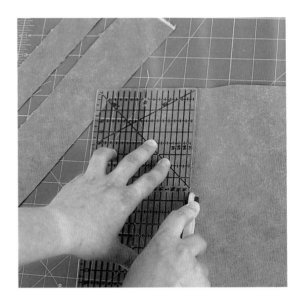

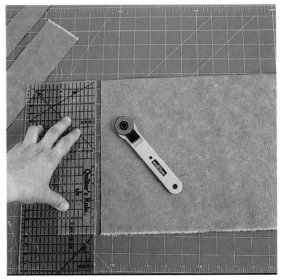

Cutting Safety

The rotary cutter has a very sharp blade and it's easy to accidentally cut yourself or others, so please follow these safety tips:

✓ Hold the cutter firmly in the same hand you write with at a 45-degree angle, and hold the ruler in place with your other hand.

✓ Cut with the blade against the side of your ruler – on the right if you are right-handed and on the left if you are left-handed. The patchwork piece you are cutting should be under the rule.

✓ Use a sharp blade that is free from nicks and other damage. Using a dull blade requires more pressure when you cut and risks the blade slipping.

✓ Stand up to cut and place the mat on a firm surface – a kitchen counter or sturdy table is ideal.

✓ Always cut away from yourself.

✓ Always replace the safety guard on the cutter, and make a habit of doing this after every cut.

✓ Wear something on your feet when you cut, in case you drop the cutter.

✓ Keep cutting equipment away from children and pets.

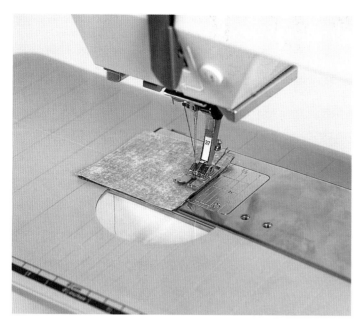

MACHINE PIECING PATCHWORK

With reference to the pictures above, place your first two pieces right sides together, making sure the edges to be sewn line up. Set your sewing machine to a slightly shorter than average stitch length and check the tension is even. Use the quarter-inch foot and line up the fabric edge with the edge of the foot when you sew. It may help if you sit slightly to the right of the machine needle so you can see this easily. Some quarter-inch feet have a guide plate on the right-hand side so the fabric can't be sewn with a wider seam.

Chain piecing is an industrial technique that speeds up piecing patchwork. When you have sewn your first two pieces together, don't cut the thread. Place the next two pieces together and sew them a stitch or two after the first two pieces. Continue like this to make a 'chain' that can be cut up afterwards (see below).

PRESSING PATCHWORK

Press each stage of your patchwork as you go along, with the seam allowance to one side as later this will help stop the wadding (batting) from 'bearding' or coming through the seam. Press towards the darker fabric out of preference, as pressing dark towards light can cause a shadow effect on paler fabrics. Pressing in alternate directions makes the seams interlock neatly when the work is assembled and avoids lumpy seams where four layers of the seam allowance meet.

Press from the front of the work with a dry iron or just a little steam, using an up and down action so the patchwork is not stretched and distorted – you should be pressing, not ironing! Good pressing can really make a difference to your patchwork and the look of the finished project so it's best to get it right before you continue piecing.

TIP

IF YOUR MACHINE TENDS TO LOOP UP THE FIRST FEW STITCHES, USE A PIECE OF SCRAP FABRIC AS A 'LEADER' WHEN YOU BEGIN AND CHAIN PIECE THE FIRST TWO PATCHWORK PIECES ON TO THAT.

SEMINOLE PATCHWORK

This machine piecing technique originated with the American Seminole Indians. It can speed up piecing patchwork made from squares and rectangles, as in the Tringle Rucksack. Seminole patchwork must be machine sewn because the seams are cut across and hand sewing would come undone.

Follow the numbered sequence below. Rotary cut strips to the required width and sew them together, first as pairs, then sew pairs together until the panel is complete – this stops the strips creeping out of alignment. Press the seams to one side. Rotary cut further units across the sewn seam, remembering the seam allowance, then rearrange and sew together. For a 4in four-patch block, you would cut strips and then the units 2½in wide. The finished block would still have a ¼in seam allowance all round, measuring 4½in.

TRIANGLE SQUARES

This speed piecing machine technique allows you to make triangle square elements in a block, as used in the Starry Backpack, without sewing on a cut bias edge, which may distort and spoil your patchwork.

Start by adding an extra ⅜in seam allowance to your two squares (e.g. 2½ + ⅜in = 2⅞in). Starting at 1 of the numbered sequence below, draw a diagonal line on the lighter square and place the squares together. Treat this line as the fabric edge, lining it up with the edge of the quarter-inch foot, and machine sew. Sew again along the other side of the drawn line and then cut along the line. Press towards the darker fabric and clip off the 'dog ears'. This makes two triangle squares. Sew two triangle squares together, repeating the method, to make a four triangle block. Blocks that use triangle squares include Birds in Flight and Pinwheel (see Block Library, page 117).

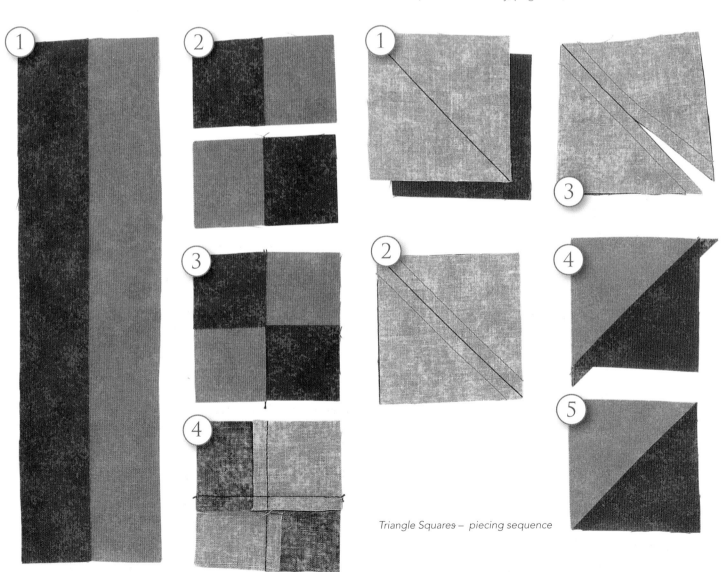

Seminole patchwork – piecing sequence

Triangle Squares – piecing sequence

FLYING GEESE

This is another machine piecing method that avoids sewing on a cut bias edge. The technique was used to create strips of Flying Geese units for the Batik Bottle Tidy.

This easy Flying Geese unit uses a rectangle (the 'goose') on a 2:1 ratio. For a 1in x 2in finished size, add ¼in seam allowance and cut a 1½in x 2½in piece. The triangle (the 'sky') is a made from a square the same size as the shortest side of the rectangle, i.e. 1½in square. Cut two squares for each rectangle. Draw a diagonal line on each square. Place one square on the rectangle and sew along the drawn line. Fold over the triangle and press. Trim away excess fabric underneath and repeat. This makes one unit. If you sew a second line ½in from the first on the excess fabric and cut between the two lines, you can make little triangle squares as you go, which can be used for another project.

Flying Geese may be sewn together in a strip, as in the Batik Bottle Tidy, and also form part of blocks such as Eight-Point Star (see the Starry Backpack). There are other ways to make Flying Geese but I find this method is good for scrap piecing.

The triangle square and Flying Geese unit methods can be used to build up other blocks, as shown at the bottom of the page – Snowball a triangle corner within a triangle square and a square on point. The Block Library on page 116 has more ideas.

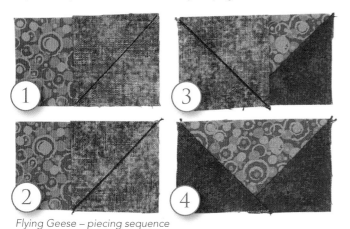

Flying Geese – piecing sequence

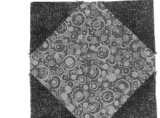

Snowball block

Triangle corner within a triangle square

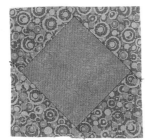

Square on point block

FOUNDATION PIECING

You can make patchwork quickly and accurately with foundation piecing. Pieces are machine sewn together on to a foundation, which stabilizes the fabric. The Quilter's Portfolio corner Log Cabin block uses a fabric foundation which is left in place as part of the bag.

Foundation piecing is a good technique for tricky fabrics that fray or stretch easily, especially permanent foundations for silk. A range of different specialized stabilizer materials are available but I used calico or muslin for the projects in this book. Press your work at each stage for a crisp finish. More complex foundation piecing often uses a paper foundation, torn away before the patchwork is quilted.

Foundation piecing – adding fabric strips to make a stitch and flip strip

STITCH AND FLIP STRIP

This method is the most basic form of foundation piecing and is an easy method for scraps and crazy patchwork too (see the Bollywood Handbag and the Crazy Patchwork Pouch). Cut a foundation strip the required width and length for your project, remembering to add the seam allowances. Cut an assortment of patchwork pieces in various widths – the length should be slightly longer than the foundation strip width. Place the first piece face up on the end of the foundation strip and line up the edges. Place the second piece face down on the first piece, pin and machine sew the two pieces together with a ¼in seam along the long edge only, through the foundation strip as well. Flip the second piece over so the right side is showing and press. Continue adding pieces in the same way until the whole foundation strip is covered. See page 103 for further advice on crazy patchwork.

LOG CABIN

The traditional Log Cabin block develops the stitching and flipping idea further. It can be made with or without a foundation fabric. Exciting effects can be achieved by varying the widths of the Log Cabin strips to make curved Log Cabin (see the Secret Pocket Sack). Corner Log Cabin begins with the first piece in one corner (see the Quilter's Portfolio) and substituting that corner square with a rectangle makes an elongated version (see the Quilter's Pocket Book).

1 Mark guidelines for Log Cabin on a fabric foundation, for example, concentric squares at 1in intervals for 1in strips. Cut strips ½in wider than the finished size. The centre square can be the same size as the strip width, in which case the first strip will be the same size as the square, or larger. Pin the centre square piece in place. Log Cabin centres in old quilts are usually a bright or light colour.

2 Pin, machine stitch and flip the first strip. Use the guidelines on the foundation to help align the strips. The Log Cabin light and dark effect is created by sewing the strips in pairs around the block. Start with light strips if you want the darker tone to predominate or vice versa.

3 Pin, machine stitch and flip the second strip. Continue adding strips in this way until the block is complete.

To sew a Log Cabin block without a foundation fabric, follow Steps 1–3 but simply omit the foundation. For an even easier method, cut the fabric strips to length as you go, machine sewing with the new strip underneath rather than on top each time. With larger blocks from many narrow strips, keep the block square and flat by using a walking foot rather than the quarter inch foot, lining up the ¼in seam with the guidelines on the machine's throat plate.

Foundation piecing for Log Cabin – adding fabric strips

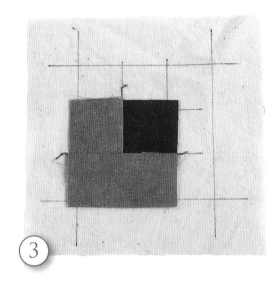

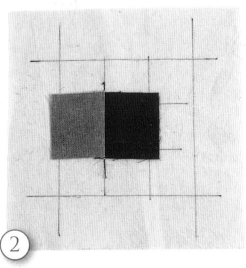

APPLIQUÉ

Appliqué involves laying and stitching one piece of fabric over another to create a decorative design and this technique is good for enhancing bag designs. Simple appliqué shapes often work best and are sewn to backing fabric by hand or machine. Appliqué is not a patchwork technique but a method in itself and there are many kinds that you can explore on your own. The techniques described below are those I used for some of the bags in this book.

Hand appliqué
This method can create exciting effects. Raw-edge hand appliqué (shown left in the picture below) is popular and produces a soft, feathery edge. It works well with tightly woven fabrics such as batiks if you don't want a very frayed look. Try using simple shapes with mostly bias edges, sewn on in running stitch or hand embroidery stitches. Cut out the shape without a seam allowance and hand or machine sew it to the background (see the Leafy Satchel).

Needleturn appliqué
This method of appliqué gives a firmer, stronger edge to the appliquéd shape (right in picture below). It uses an appliqué needle or a long sharp to turn under the turning allowance as you sew, using the point of the needle to stroke it into place (see circular picture below). Cut out the shape with a ⅛in turning allowance all round and tack (baste) the shape to the background with small stitches ¼in from the cut edge. The tacking stitches prevent too much fabric being turned under. Work with the edge of the appliqué towards you, so you can see your stitches. As most of the appliqué shape will have a bias edge, it is not necessary to clip the fabric on a curve, just ease it under. Only clip into deep V-shapes and then only a few threads of fabric. Press the turned edge between your fingers as you go along. Start and finish sewing on a long side, sewing the shape to the background with small hemming stitches. For the Secret Pocket Sack, I used an easy method for appliqué circles – see Step 3 on page 57.

Raw-edge appliqué   *Needleturn appliqué*

CRAZY PATCHWORK

Taking the foundation piecing idea one step further and mixing it with appliqué produces crazy patchwork, a Victorian technique from the 1870s that is very popular today. Scraps of fabric, ribbon and lace are appliquéd to a foundation fabric and embellished with embroidery stitches, buttons and beads – in fact, almost anything that can be sewn on! Because the foundation fabric does the job of supporting everything, different kinds of fabrics can be combined, such as silks and velvets. Crazy patchwork can also be made with fused appliqué, by ironing a fusible web to the back of the fabric scraps, although this stiffens the fabrics slightly. I used several variations of crazy patchwork in this book.

Random Log Cabin/ stitch and flip
(see the Crazy Patchwork Pouch) Starting from the centre, strips of various fabrics and ribbons were machine sewn to the foundation, each one overlapping the raw edge of a previous strip, flipped and pressed. The foundation fabric was trimmed to size after the patchwork was complete and hand embroidery stitches added over each seam.

Raw-edge crazy patchwork
(see the Luscious Berry Bag) Starting from the centre, raw-edge strips and scraps were machine appliquéd, with various decorative machine stitches overlapping the raw edges, to make a rectangle of patchwork. This was further embellished with simple machine embroidery before the bag panels were cut.

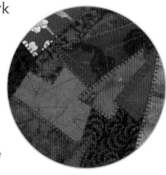

Raw-edge crazy patchwork
variation (see the Pudding Bag) Starting at the outer edge, rectangles and wedge shapes were machine appliquéd with the same decorative machine stitch and thread used throughout. The patches spiralled into the centre, overlapping the previous patches, the final patch covering the last raw edges. If the patches were cut with bias edges, they could be appliquéd with a straight machine stitch for a ragged-edge effect.

Quilting Techniques

This section describes how to mark out a quilting pattern, make a quilt sandwich and quilt the patchwork blocks or the fabric panels of your bags. Quilting may be sewn by hand or machine, each method giving a different effect (see photos opposite page). Only the patchwork or appliqué parts of the bags in this book are quilted – the plain fabrics, such as denim or faux suede, are left plain.

Making a quilt 'sandwich' of fabric, wadding and backing

Marking a Quilting Pattern

Before you start quilting, you may need to mark the quilting pattern. Use a suitable marker that can be removed later. The bag quilting designs fall into several groups and some do not need marking. You can also invent your own patterns. If you are planning to machine quilt the design, patterns with continuous lines are easier as there is less stopping and starting and fewer ends to finish off.

• Quilt along patchwork seam lines, called quilting 'in the ditch', or following the fabric print – neither require marking (see the Log Cabin Saddlebag).

• Quilt simple straight lines and zigzags, sometimes without marking or with minimal marking. Use a quilter's ruler and marker to draw straight lines directly on the fabric as required. Lines can be quilted in embroidery stitches (see the Glitter Pouch, page 31).

• Quilt wavy lines and simple motifs freehand (see the Leafy Satchel). Patterns can be improvized or drawn directly on to the fabric. Free motion quilted wiggly lines, known as stipple or vermicelli quilting, look remarkably effective (see the machine quilting in the circular photo, right).

Making a Quilt Sandwich

After marking the quilt pattern you can prepare the quilt sandwich. Press the patchwork and backing fabric. Place the backing right side down on a flat surface and use masking tape to tape it down. Lay the wadding (batting) on top and smooth it out. Remember to match your wadding to the quilting technique you want to use – some wadding made for machine quilting is not suitable for hand quilting and vice versa (see waddings, page 94). Place the patchwork on top, making sure there is wadding and backing behind all the patchwork. Tack (baste) the three layers together, working from the centre outwards in a radiating pattern. This method is suitable for the small pieces of quilting used in bags. Diagonal tacking anchors the layers

together even more firmly and is easier to remove after machine quilting (see Stitch Library, page 112). Alternatively, pin the layers together, but take care when machine sewing over pins. Once the quilt sandwich has been prepared, you are ready to quilt – machine quilting and hand quilting techniques are described below and on the following pages.

Machine Quilting

Machine quilting (see photo, right) produces a distinct line which can be used to emphasize the patchwork by quilting 'in the ditch' or along the patchwork seam line, on the other side of the seam from the patchwork seam allowance. Machine quilt with a darker thread in a graphic style (see the Retro Traveller, page 79) or use invisible nylon thread if you don't want to see the stitches. If your machine has embroidery or interesting utility stitches, experiment with these for quilting (see the Pudding Bag). Some machines have a half speed feature which slows the stitching down and a 'needle down' selection option – both are useful.

You can machine quilt with the machine feed dogs set 'up', a walking foot and quilt in straight or gently curved lines. Working from the top, the walking foot helps to evenly feed all the layers through the machine at the same rate, working in unison with the feed dogs. Unlike quilting a large quilt, which usually begins in the centre, starting and finishing at the edge of a small patchwork means there are fewer loose ends to finish off. Make sure the needle is down in the fabric before raising the presser foot to turn corners. Follow gentle curves by raising the presser foot and turning the fabric slightly after every couple of stitches. This method is best for quilting in the ditch and straight lines (see the Starry Backpack).

Free-motion machine quilting is useful for more decorative patterns but requires practice, as the feed dogs are set 'down' and you need to control the fabric feeding through the machine yourself. Bags are great for practice pieces! With a darning or quilting foot and the stitch length set to zero, you can move your work in any direction. You may need to re-thread the bobbin to

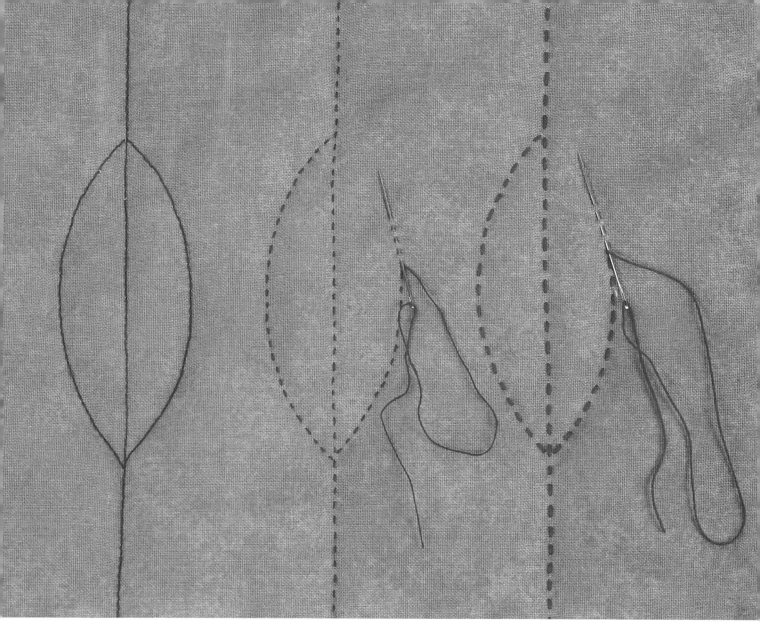

Machine quilting

Hand quilting

Big stitch quilting

Machine quilting with walking foot

Free-motion machine quilting

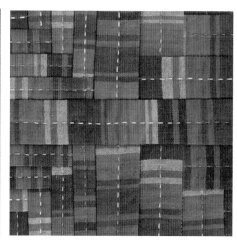

Big stitch quilting

achieve a tighter bobbin tension – check your machine manual. Wearing a pair of gloves with rubber grips on them (gardening gloves or the quilters' version) will help you control the fabric. This method is best for decorative machine quilting (see the Party Party bag, page 41) and is essential for stipple quilting, also known as vermicelli.

Newer machines can stitch on the spot to finish off the thread ends or you could sew the last few stitches with a very short stitch length. In these bags, the back of the quilting is always hidden by the lining or bag construction, so loose ends can be pulled through to the back and knotted off.

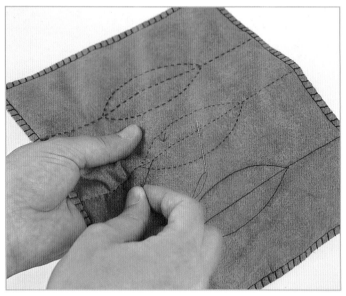

Starting hand quilting

HAND QUILTING

Hand quilting (centre in the large photo on previous page) gives a softer appearance than machine quilting. The aim is to have evenly spaced stitches rather than really tiny ones (see starting hand quilting, below). Traditional quilting in a frame helps to keep the layers taut and the quilting even. I don't use a frame to quilt bags as the patchwork pieces are small and are easier to work in the hand. If you want to use a frame, machine tack (baste) scrap pieces of fabric to each edge of the piece you want to quilt, so you have fabric to anchor the work in the frame. There are various kinds of smaller quilting frames and hoops available, some with clips to hold the work in place. Needles for hand quilting are called betweens and are smaller than sharps. If you work without a frame, you may find a small sharp easier to use but make sure your tension doesn't pucker up your quilting.

Big Stitch Quilting
'Big stitch' is a variation on hand quilting, using thicker thread and larger stitches (right in large photo on previous page). Use a crewel or embroidery needle suitable for the thread. Big stitch can enhance the colours in your patchwork and introduce multicoloured threads or metallics in an interesting way.

Starting hand quilting
Cut a thread about 18in long (shorter for embroidery threads and metallics) and tie a knot in one end, leaving a 'tail' about ½in long. Thread the needle. Insert the needle into the front of the work about ¾in along the line you are going to quilt and bring the needle up to start stitching. Gently pull the knot through the fabric and into the wadding (batting) and start stitching along the line. The 'tail' will be following the quilted line and this will be anchored by your first few stitches. Take small, neat stitches – loading just three or four stitches on the needle keeps straight lines straight.

Finishing hand quilting
Make a knot about ¼in from the fabric surface. Take a backstitch, insert the needle along the line you have quilted and pull the knot through into the wadding (batting). For extra secure finishing, tie two knots ¼in apart, these are very unlikely to work their way out of the quilting.

Neaten the edges of patchwork panels after quilting, before assembling your bag, by overlocking – check your machine for suitable stitches.

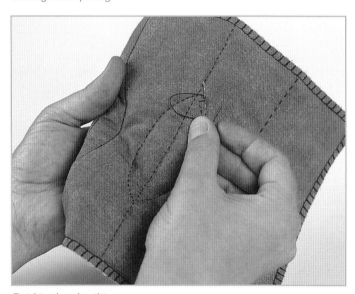

Finishing hand quilting

Matching quilting threads to needles
Match the type of quilting thread you want to use to your needle for best results.

Thread Type	Needle Type
Cotton hand quilting thread	Between or sharp
Embroidery threads (perlé, flower thread etc.)	Crewel or embroidery
Metallic embroidery threads	Crewel
Machine quilting	Medium universal or quilting
Jeans topstitch (machine)	Jeans
Rayon embroidery (machine)	Embroidery
Metallic embroidery (machine)	Metallic

Bag Making Techniques

Once your patchwork and quilting is complete you can assemble your bag. Project instructions give details while this section describes the general bag making techniques required, including binding fabric edges, inserting zips, creating straps and making linings.

Making and Attaching Bindings

It is quite easy to make your own straight or bias bindings to co-ordinate with or match your bag. Use straight bindings (cut from the straight grain) where a firm straight edge is needed, such as the top of a pocket. Use bias binding where the edge has curves or curved corners. Double bindings are easiest to make and sew and are stronger in wear than single bindings. Take care not to stretch bias binding when easing around corners. Bias strips can also be used to make co-ordinated covered piping.

1 Cut 2in wide fabric strips to the length required. Straight grain strips will have a little stretch if cut across the fabric, from selvage to selvage. Cut bias strips at 45 degrees, using the 45-degree angle on your quilter's ruler. Larger bags will require joining pieces of binding. Both straight and bias bindings should be joined at a 45-degree angle (see below). Cross the two strips and mark a stitching line, then machine sew. Trim off the excess fabric and press the seam open.

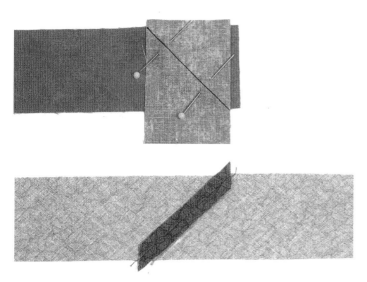

2 Fold the binding almost in half lengthways and press the fold in place. This way both raw edges of the binding are visible as it is pinned and sewn in place, so any puckers in the fabric underneath can be eased out. Clip off the 'dog ears'.

3 When attaching binding, pin the binding to the edge of the patchwork panel, raw edge to raw edge, as described in the individual bag project. Set the bias binding slightly back from the patchwork edge, so all the layers are visible and any puckers can be eased out. Machine sew the binding in place, leaving about 4in of binding unsewn at the start and finish to make joining easier. Open out the folded binding and join the ends with a 45-degree angle, as in Step 1. Refold the binding and finish sewing it to the panel.

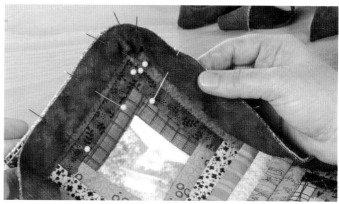

4 Turn the binding to the back and stitch down using blind hemming stitch. Take care not to twist the binding.

Inserting Zips

Some of the bags have zip fasteners, inserted by three basic methods. The visible method is good for chunky zips (such as the Retro Traveller, page 79). A variation on this method (shown below), where part of the lining is sewn in at the same time as the zip, is used for the Tringle Rucksack and the Secret Pocket Sack. Use the invisible method, used in dressmaking, where the zip is sewn into the main part of the bag (the Log Cabin Saddlebag) or an inner zipped pocket (the Crazy Patchwork Pouch).

Tack (baste) zips in place with diagonal tacking as it is easier to remove after machine stitching. Bar tacks at either end of zips make it more secure (see Stitch Library, page 112). Allow ½in seam allowances for zips. Machine sew with a zipper foot to allow stitching close to the zip teeth. Take care not to sew over the teeth, which can break the needle. I sew with the zip open whenever possible. Stop sewing at the zip pull with the needle down in the fabric, draw the pull past the part being sewn and continue stitching. Zips can also be hand sewn.

Inserting a visible zip

1 With reference to the three pictures below, fold under the first piece of fabric ½in and pin it to the zip. The folded edge should be close to the teeth but allow the zip to be unfastened. Machine sew down the edge about ⅛in from the fold. Sew the second piece of fabric to the zip the same way.

2 Cut fabric to equal the total width of the zip gusset. Machine sew this to the end of the zip gusset.

3 Cut fabric for the other end of the zip gusset and machine sew. Press end pieces outwards. Trim the gusset to the required length. See the the Tringle Rucksack (page 71) for instructions on sewing in part of the lining at the same time as the zip.

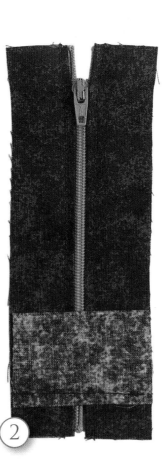

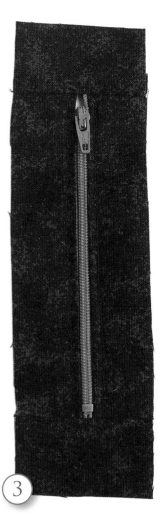

Inserting a visible zip

① ② ③

Inserting a zip invisibly

1 With a ½in seam allowance, machine (or hand) sew both ends of the zip gusset, starting and finishing with backstitches. Tack (baste) the remaining opening closed.

2 Press the seam open and then diagonally tack the zip in place from the back.

3 Machine (or hand) sew the zip from the right side of work, removing tacking (basting) and opening the zip as required. Check that the zip opens and remove tacking holding it in place. The ends of the zip opening can be reinforced with a bar tack (see Stitch Library page 112).

Inserting a zip invisibly

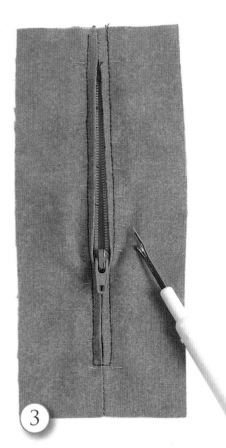

(1) (2) (3)

Calculating fabric sizes for zip gussets

If you want to adapt a bag you may need to change the size of the zip gusset using the information here (see also Adapting bags, page 111).

For a bag with a visible zip gusset:

Long pieces (cut 2):
To calculate the length of the fabric: add ½in to the length of the zip.

To calculate the width of the fabric: subtract the width of the zip teeth (approx ¼in) from the width of gusset, divide by 2 and add ¾in (¼in normal seam allowance and ½in for zip edge).

End pieces (cut 2):
To calculate the length of the fabric: subtract the length of the zip gusset after Step 1 from the desired finished length, divide the result by 2 and add ¾in.

To calculate the width of the fabric: measure the width of the zip gusset after Step 1.

For a bag with an unlined visible zip gusset:

Long pieces (cut 2):
To calculate the length of the fabric: (to be folded in half lengthways at start of Step 1) add ½in to the length of the zip tape.

To calculate the width of the fabric: subtract the width of the zip teeth (approximately ¼in) from the width of the gusset and add ½in.

End pieces (cut 2):
As for visible zip gusset, or cut four and sew a piece to each side of the zip gusset in Steps 2 and 3 to conceal all raw edges when finished.

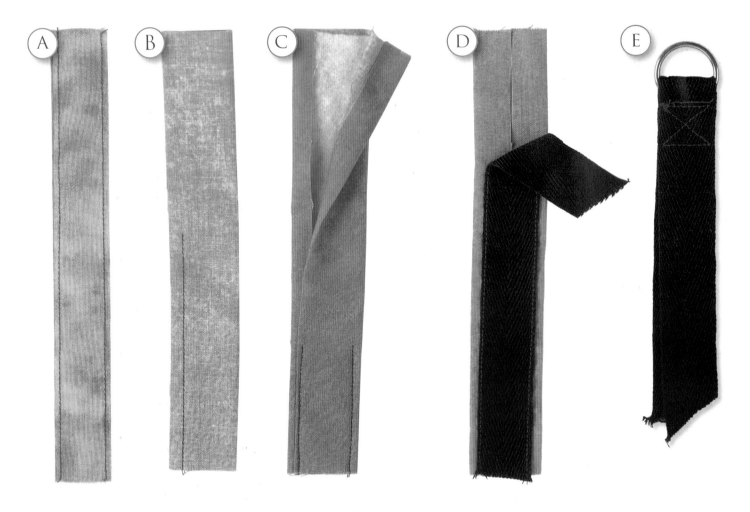

Making Straps

The most basic strap is a single piece of strong webbing. Four other strap methods use fabric to match the bag. Remember that fabric tends to stretch across the grain, from selvage to selvage, so always cut the strap parallel to the selvage.

Basic strap (A)

This method is given in the stepped instructions for the Quilters' Pocket Book on page 24. The piece of fabric needs to be cut to the actual finished length (remember to allow for sewing the strap to the bag or D-rings) and four times the finished width of the strap. It may be backed with iron-on interfacing for extra strength. Machine sew each strap, sewing one line very close to each long edge. Add more parallel stitching lines if you wish.

Tube strap (B)

Cut a strip of fabric to the desired length (finished length + ½in) and width (double the finished width + ½in). Fold the fabric wrong sides together and machine sew along one side. Turn the strap right side out and press with the seam to one side. Narrow straps in thick fabric or with wadding (batting) are more difficult to turn right side out.

Padded strap (C)

Cut fabric as if making a tube strap and cut a strip of wadding (batting) the same size as the finished length and width. Tack (baste) the wadding to the fabric, ¼in from the long edge, fold the fabric over and machine sew in place. Remove the tacking.

Folded strap (D)

This method can be used for webbing that would be too thin to use on its own. Cut a strip of fabric to the desired length (finished length + ½in) and double the finished width, which must be the same as or wider than the webbing. Cut a piece of webbing the same length as the fabric. Fold the fabric edges towards the centre and press in place. Now machine sew the webbing along the length of the strap.

Attaching straps and D-rings (E)

Straps can be sewn directly to a bag (see the Batik Bottle Tidy), attached with D-rings or D-rings and snaps (see the Log Cabin Saddlebag). Attach the strap securely by machine sewing a figure of eight. To sew the strap directly to a bag, fold under the ends of the strap and stitch. If the strap is quite thick, the fold may be omitted and the strap ends covered with a piece of appliqué. The bag can also be reinforced at this point with a piece of strong calico on the inside. Use the same figure of eight stitching to attach the straps to D-rings and clips. Thread the strap through the D-ring or the bar on the clip, fold the raw edge under and machine sew.

MAKING LININGS

All the bags in this book have linings. The basic linings, without pockets, are cut to the same sizes as the outer bag panels. The easiest way to cut the linings accurately is to use the outer panels as cutting patterns, before the bag is assembled. Very thin lining fabrics, such as waterproof nylon, may be semi-transparent and will need an interlining sewn to the back. Slipstitching the lining to the bag along the seam lines, working from inside the bag, helps to keep the lining in place at the top of the Bollywood Handbag. Topstitching around the edge of bags like the Tuck-in bag keeps the join between bag and lining crisply folded.

ADDING EXTRA POCKETS

Many of the bags have pockets and the various types used are described in the projects but if you wish to add extra pockets or customize your bag interior or further adapt the designs, the following advice should help.

To add an extra pocket, first make a sketch of the bag outer or lining, note the dimensions and mark where you would like to add the pocket.

To make a pocket the same width as your lining, follow the assembly directions for the Crazy Patchwork Pouch lining on page 30. Cut the pocket as wide as the lining and any length you wish, shorter than the side of the bag.

To make a self-lined patch pocket, decide the size of the pocket and cut out an extra piece of lining twice that size. Fold it in half, right sides together and sew around the edge leaving a 2in gap. Bag out, slipstitch the gap closed and machine sew the patch pocket to the lining, reinforcing the lining behind the pocket stitching with a piece of calico slightly larger than the pocket.

To insert zip pockets in the lining, follow the directions for the Crazy Patchwork Pouch on page 30. Remember that the pocket fabric will be the same width as the lining. If you want a lot of pockets, like the folded pockets inside the Quilter's Pocket Book or the Crazy Patchwork Pouch (shown below), split the lining up into different elements. Divide your lining plan into rectangles and squares, rather like making an asymmetric patchwork block and think of each element like a piece for patchwork. Add the pockets to each piece and assemble the lining like a patchwork, sewing the edges of the pockets into the lining seams. In this way you can add pockets for specific items, such as notebooks, pencils, membership cards or keys.

Adapting bags

Part of the fun of making bags is adapting them to suit your own needs and design ideas, so you will have created a truly unique and useful accessory.

• Change fabric themes and patchwork designs. Refer to Fabric Themes on pages 114 and 115 for ideas. There are also suggestions for patchwork blocks in the Block Library on pages 116 and 117.

• Add extra pockets or simplify pocket arrangements (see instructions, left).

• Change the length and width of straps, or the type of strap used (see page 110).

• Use different trims and fasteners and remember to co-ordinate metallic finishes.

• Make the bag bigger or smaller. Decide how large you would like it to be, remembering to think three-dimensionally. Making a sketch and drawing a plan on squared paper helps. If a bag is for your cutting mat, quilter's ruler or sketchbook, check the size. Unless stated otherwise, the fabric requirements in the bag instructions are given without seam allowances to make resizing easier, so remember to add seam allowances when you cut out the pieces. Mark the position and size of patchwork panels on your plan and list the dimensions of all the pieces – this will be your cutting list. You may also need to change the length of zips and straps. Several bags have curved corners sewn to a gusset, so check the circumference of the curve and allow for this when calculating the length of the gusset panels. The original bag assembly instructions may need to be amended with extra steps, if you wish add a pocket for example, so read through them and make a note of where you need to add an extra construction step. The Crazy Patchwork Pouch and the Luscious Berry Bag may be scaled up or down by using a photocopier and the measurements of the Retro Traveller variation bag are the original ones multiplied by three. Use the completed outer panels as patterns to cut the lining, so you can be sure the lining will fit.

Enjoy making your bags!

STITCH LIBRARY

Various hand stitches were used in the construction of the bags including backstitch, bar tacking, diagonal tacking, general tacking (basting), hemming stitch, herringbone stitch and running stitch. Decorative embroidery stitches were used for embellishment on some of the bags. I used machine embroidery but you may prefer to embroider by hand and so stitch diagrams for blanket stitch, chain stitch, feather stitch, fly stitch, stem stitch and whipped running stitch are included here.

BACKSTITCH

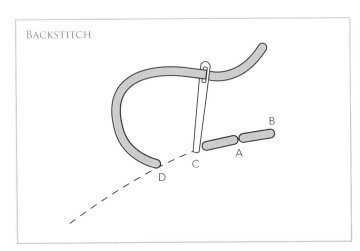

BAR TACKING

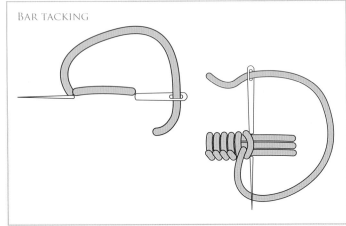

BLANKET STITCH

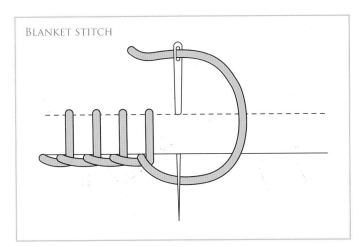

CHAIN STITCH

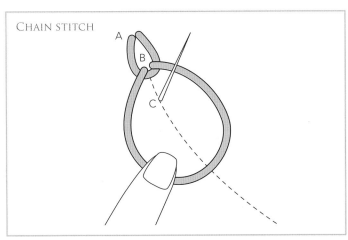

DIAGONAL TACKING

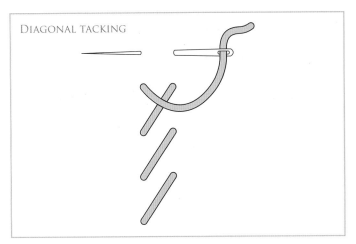

FEATHER STITCH

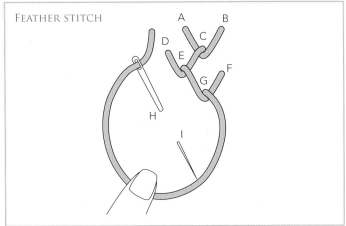

FLY STITCH

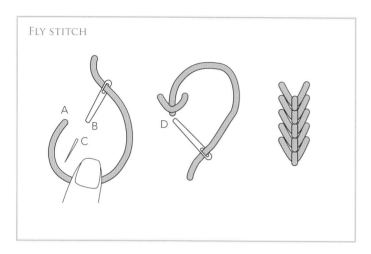

HERRINGBONE STITCH

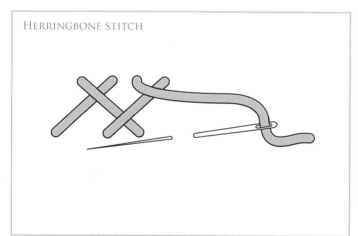

WHIPPED RUNNING STITCH

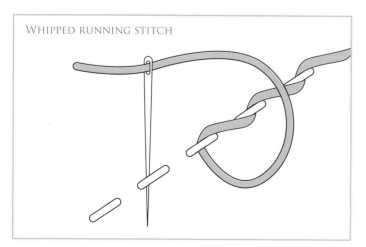

HEMMING STITCH

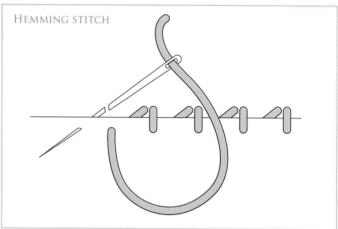

STEM STITCH

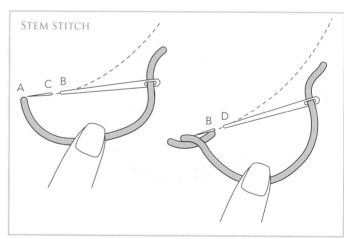

WHIPSTITCH OR OVERSEWING

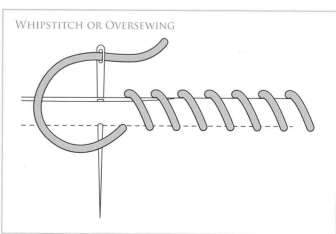

FABRIC THEMES

Bags are excellent for trying out new fabric colours and themes or you can use up fabrics from your scrap bag. As an experiment with new fabrics or novelty prints they are ideal, as you don't have the commitment of a larger project. Lightweight furnishing fabrics, denim, leather and suede (real or faux) can be included where piecing is not required. Enhance your theme by careful selection of buttons and other notions, matching metallic finishes for a professional finish. Big stitch quilting, embroidery, beads and trims can further embellish your bags. I used ten themes in this book.

BATIK BRIGHTS – COLOURFUL

FLYING GEESE, TRIANGLE SQUARES AND PINWHEEL BLOCKS IN A BURST OF TROPICAL BRILLIANCE, ACCENTED WITH DEEP BLUES

INDIA – EXOTIC

NEUTRALS CONTRAST WITH GLOWING SILKS, GLITTERING GOLD AND SHISHA MIRRORS

COOL BLUES – CASUAL

TRADITIONAL BLOCKS IN FADED DENIM AND SHIRT CHECKS FOR RELAXED, CLASSIC JEANS STYLING

RETRO FIFTIES – CHIC

1950S CONTEMPORARY STYLE WITH SPIKEY PATCHWORK STARS AND GRAPHIC QUILTING ACCENTS

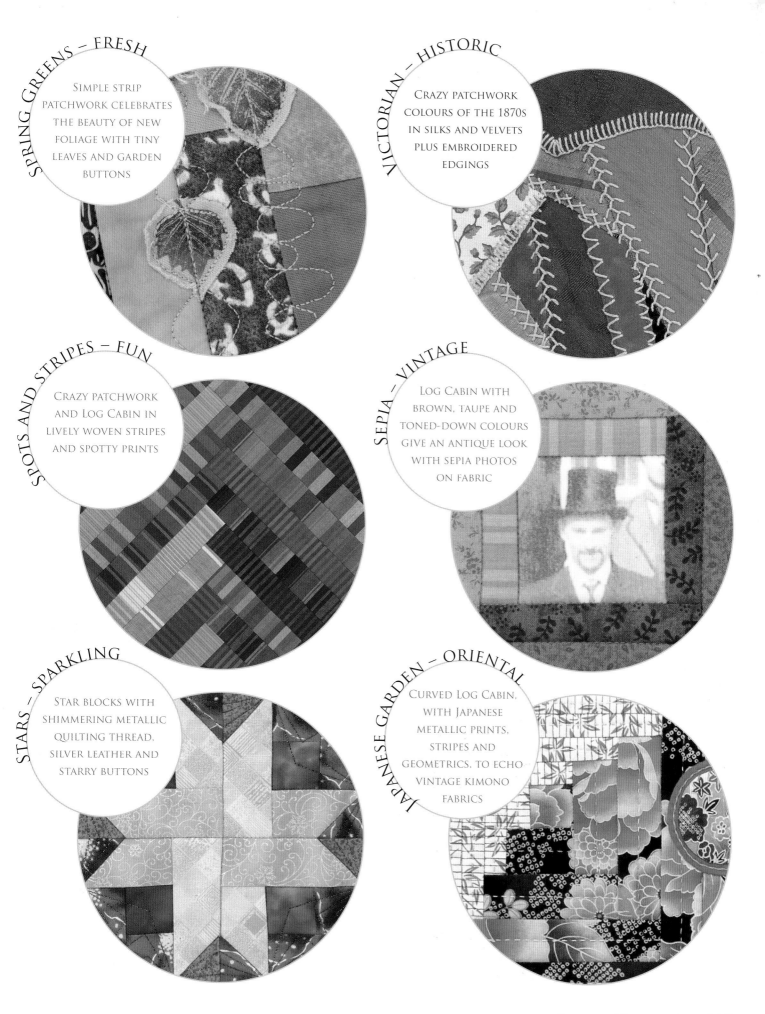

SPRING GREENS – FRESH

SIMPLE STRIP PATCHWORK CELEBRATES THE BEAUTY OF NEW FOLIAGE WITH TINY LEAVES AND GARDEN BUTTONS

VICTORIAN – HISTORIC

CRAZY PATCHWORK COLOURS OF THE 1870s IN SILKS AND VELVETS PLUS EMBROIDERED EDGINGS

SPOTS AND STRIPES – FUN

CRAZY PATCHWORK AND LOG CABIN IN LIVELY WOVEN STRIPES AND SPOTTY PRINTS

SEPIA – VINTAGE

LOG CABIN WITH BROWN, TAUPE AND TONED-DOWN COLOURS GIVE AN ANTIQUE LOOK WITH SEPIA PHOTOS ON FABRIC

STARS – SPARKLING

STAR BLOCKS WITH SHIMMERING METALLIC QUILTING THREAD, SILVER LEATHER AND STARRY BUTTONS

JAPANESE GARDEN – ORIENTAL

CURVED LOG CABIN, WITH JAPANESE METALLIC PRINTS, STRIPES AND GEOMETRICS, TO ECHO VINTAGE KIMONO FABRICS

BLOCK LIBRARY

This library includes some useful blocks, made with combinations of various patchwork techniques described in the previous pages, to give you more design options. The blocks here have been reduced in size to fit the page. Scale them up easily on graph paper to the size you want and make a cutting list for each block, so you have all the pieces to hand when you start sewing your patchwork. The blocks are grouped into four-patch and nine-patch designs.

Four-patch blocks are easiest to use where the finished block size can be divided by two, so 4in, 6in and 8in blocks are easy to make (these are the finished sizes, when the block is sewn into a larger patchwork).

Nine-patch blocks are suited to finished sizes divisible by three. It's possible to use four- and nine-patch designs in various sizes that don't divide so easily but you will then have individual pieces sized in fractions. For example, Eight-Point Star (shown in the exploded diagram below) works well in various sizes – the finished sizes for the corner squares would be 1in for a 4in block, 1½in for a 6in block and 2in for an 8in block (cut sizes would be 1½in, 2in and 2½in respectively).

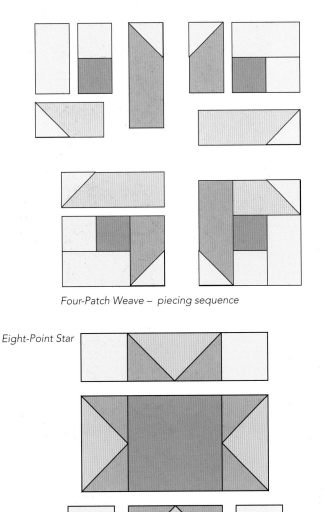

Four-Patch Weave – piecing sequence

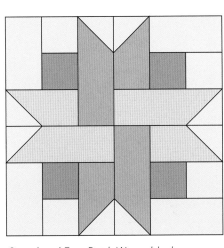

Completed Four-Patch Weave block

Eight-Point Star

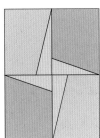

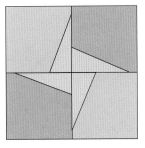

Four-Patch Star – make each point by sewing a fabric strip to the base square on an angle as shown, and then trim to match the square. To create an elongated star, start with four rectangles rather than squares

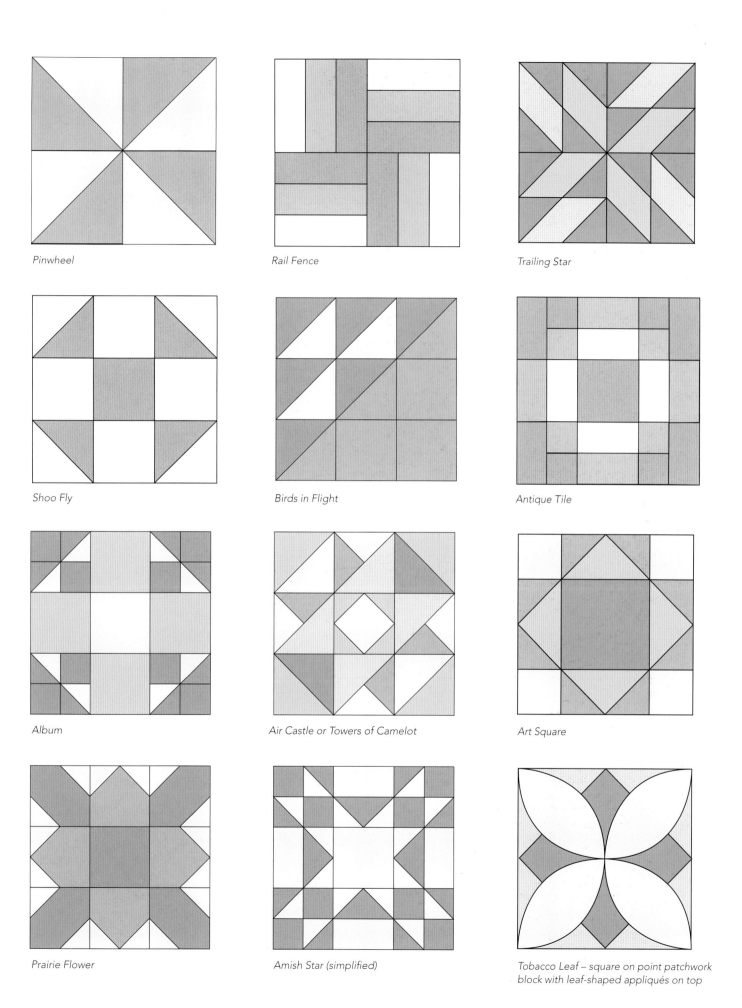

Pinwheel

Rail Fence

Trailing Star

Shoo Fly

Birds in Flight

Antique Tile

Album

Air Castle or Towers of Camelot

Art Square

Prairie Flower

Amish Star (simplified)

Tobacco Leaf – square on point patchwork block with leaf-shaped appliqués on top

MAIL-ORDER SUPPLIERS

Fabrics, notions and equipment like those used for the bags in this book are available from the following suppliers:

UK

Rustic Angel Quilts
The Byre, Greenlands Farm, Moulsford, Oxfordshire, OX10 9JT
Tel: 01491 875105
Email: rusticangelquilts@btinternet.com
www.rusticangelquilts.co.uk
For reproduction and country fabrics

The Button Lady
16 Hollyfield Road South, Sutton Coldfield,
West Midlands B76 1NX
Tel: 0121 329 3234
www.thebuttonlady.co.uk
For buttons (including wooden ones), clasps, charms, beads, sequins and soft leather pieces

The Cotton Patch
1285 Stratford Road, Hall Green, Birmingham B28 9AJ
Tel: 0121 702 2840
Email: mailorder@cottonpatch.net
www.cottonpatch.co.uk
For fabrics (including woven stripes) and patchwork supplies

Euro Japan Links Limited
32 Nant Road, Child's Hill, London NW1 2AT
Tel: 020 8201 9324
Email: eurojpn@aol.com
www.eurojapanlinks.co.uk
For Japanese fabrics and threads (Internet and mail-order only)

Glitterati Handicrafts
Suite 9, Unit 1, Staples Corner Business Park,
1000 North Circular Road, London NW2 7JP
Tel: 0208 208 2232
www.glitterati2001@aol.com
For glittery fabrics, sequined braids, exotic threads, sparkly Indian trims and shisha mirrors

Hannah's Room
50 Church Street, Brierley, Barnsley, South Yorkshire S72 9HT
Tel: 01226 713427
Email: sales@hannahsroom.co.uk
www.hannahsroom.co.uk
For batik fabrics

Patchwork Corner
51 Belswains Lane, Hemel Hempstead, Hertfordshire, HP3 9PW
Tel: 01442 259000

Email: jenny@patchworkcorner.co.uk
www.patchworkcorner.co.uk
For fabrics, bag notions and patchwork supplies

Rio Designs
Flint Cottage, Treacle Lane, Rushden, Buntingford
Hertfordshire SG9 0SL
Tel: 01763 288234
Email:sales@riodesigns.co.uk
www.riodesigns.co.uk
For computer fabric printing supplies and software

Stef Francis
Waverley, Higher Roscombe, Stokeinteignhead,
Newton Abbot, Devon TQ12 4QL
Tel: 01803 323004
www.stef-francis.co.uk
For hand-dyed threads, fabrics and trims

USA

Connecting Threads
13118 NE 4th Street, Vancouver, WA 98684
Tel: 1 800 574 6454
Email: customerservice@connectingthreads.com
www.connectingthreads.com
For general needlework and quilting supplies

eQuilter.com
5455 Spine Road, Suite E; Boulder, CO 80301 USA
Tel: USA Toll Free: 877-FABRIC-3 or: 303-527-0856
Email: service@equilter.com
www.eQuilter.com
For patchwork fabrics

Jo-ann Stores, Inc *(mail order and stores across US)*
5555 Darrow Road, Hudson, OH 44236
Tel: 1 888 739 4120
Email: guest.service@jo-annstores.com
www.joann.com
For needlework and quilting supplies

Keepsake Quilting
Route 25B, Center Harbor, NH 03226
Tel: 1 800 865 9458
Email: customerservice@keepsakequilting.com
www.keepsakequilting.com
For general needlework and quilting supplies

ACKNOWLEDGMENTS

I would like to thank everyone who contributed to the creation of *21 Sensational Patchwork Bags*. Special thanks to all the team at David & Charles who have been great to work with once again. I am grateful to Pat Morris for stitching help with bag assembly and Guy Colyer for general assistance at the step-by-step photo shoots. Many thanks to Karl Adamson, my excellent step-by-step photographer. Thank you again to Bernina – my Virtuosa 153 Quilter's Edition sewing machine stitched everything beautifully! Finally, thank you to my family and all my friends in patchwork and quilting for your support and encouragement. I hope you enjoy this book and enjoy making the bags.

ABOUT THE AUTHOR

Susan Briscoe writes and designs for patchwork and quilting magazines, and teaches patchwork and sashiko quilting. An arts graduate of the University of Wales, Aberystwyth, she started quilting in 1992, after becoming interested in patchwork while living in Japan. Susan is the author of *21 Terrific Patchwork Bags* and *The Ultimate Sashiko Soucebook*, both published by David & Charles. Susan lives in North Wales, UK.

INDEX